Der Führer

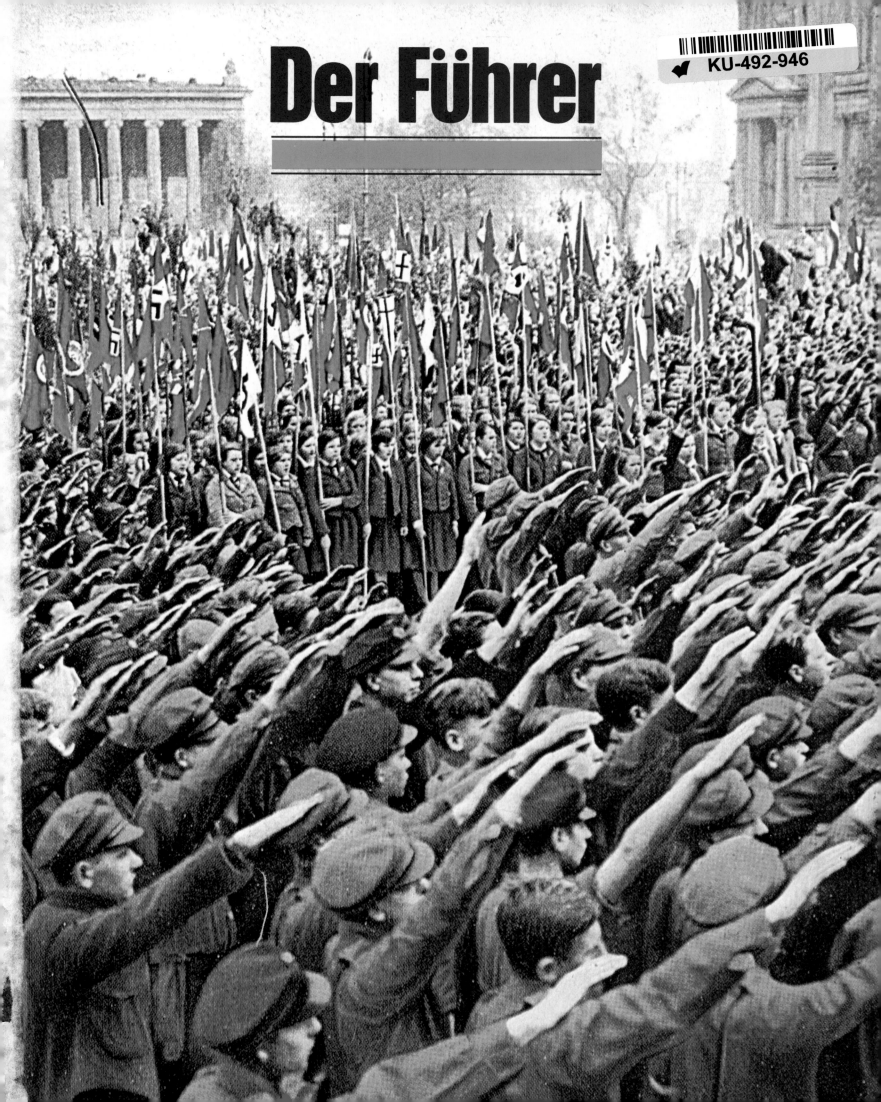

Der Führer

Edited by Herbert Walther

Bison Books

Copyright © 1978 Bison Books Limited
All rights reserved
ISBN: 0–86124–017–0
Published by Bison Books Limited
4 Cromwell Place, London SW7
Second impression 1979
Printed in Hong Kong

Contents

Herbert Walther joined the Waffen SS in 1940 and served on several fronts throughout the war until his capture in Normandy in 1944. For over eleven years he developed the picture library at the Bundesarchiv in Koblenz and provided many of the rare photographs which appear in this book.

Ward Rutherford was brought up in Jersey, where he experienced the Nazi occupation for five years. He has had extensive experience as a producer and a broadcaster for both BBC and independent television and has written ten books on a variety of subjects, the latest being *Hitler's Propaganda Machine*.

S. L. Mayer was educated at the University of Michigan and Yale University and served for twelve years as a professor of history and international relations at the University of Maryland and the University of Southern California. He has written and edited over twenty books, many of them dealing with World War II.

In 1938, as a result of Hitler's seizure of Austria in March and annexation of Czechoslovakia's Sudetenland following the Munich Conference in September, *Time* Magazine named Adolf Hitler Man of the Year. Looking back on the course of the 20th century, now more than three-quarters past, Hitler could still be regarded as the man of the century. It is not merely because he dominated Europe and world history for the twelve years he held power in Germany. It is not merely because he, more than anyone else, created the Second World War and is considered by most observers today to have been responsible for the slaughter of millions of people both on and off the battlefield. It is because Hitler's shadow looms over our own times as a colossus. To one degree or another political movements today reject the horror of Nazi Germany and the theses Hitler and the Nazi Party held to be truth. Underlying the Nazi regime were three principles which have all provoked a negative reaction.

At the heart of Hitler's philosophy, as expressed in *Mein Kampf* and thousands of his subsequent pronouncements and speeches, was the belief that the Jews were the cause of the world's and particularly Germany's troubles. To eradicate this 'foreign' element in the social body of the Third Reich, restrictions of various kinds were placed on Germany's Jews, many of whose antecedents had lived in Central Europe since Roman times or for about 2000 years. Starting with Crystal Night, when hundreds of Jewish synagogues and shops were destroyed or desecrated, Germany's Jews, at least those who still remained, were herded into concentra-

tion camps. By 1938 some three-quarters of Germany's 600,000 Jews had left the Reich for France, America, Britain or Holland, some of whom were to be caught in the Nazi net when the Wehrmacht stormed into Western Europe. Once Poland had been conquered in 1939, another three million Jews were under the swastika. By 1940, well over a million more. By 1942, at the height of Hitler's conquest of Russia, perhaps an additional four million, including those Jews who lived in the puppet or satellite states, like Hungary and Rumania. As the war progressed most of these Jews, as well as thousands of French, Poles, gypsies and other 'undesirables' were placed in concentration camps, many of which were organized as extermination camps, where tortures of a hideous nature were practiced on the Nazis' victims. Some nine million people were killed in Nazi concentration camps and of these approximately six million were Jews.

What was the world's reaction to this abominable act against humanity? First of all, sympathy went out to Europe's remaining Jewish population and to the attempt to establish a Jewish state in the Levant. Once the state of Israel was established in 1948, most of Europe and North America supported its existence, a support which, to a greater or lesser degree, continues today. Secondly, the world's revulsion against racist theories led to the decolonization of Asia and Africa as well as a universal belief that equality of treatment for all peoples, whatever their race or religious views, was a *sine qua non* of every civilized government. Although this view was espoused but not practiced in Eastern Europe

Work, Bread and Freedom – an early Nazi slogan.

These were the building blocks of the Third Reich.

Far left: A parade passes Hitler's birthplace in Braunau, Austria. Hitler was born there on 20 April 1889.
Left: Nazis parade in Munich in 1923 bearing the Kaiser's flag.

after the war, and not espoused at all in places like South Africa, it is fair to say that movements such as the equality of opportunity given to blacks in the United States or the free movement of peoples throughout the British Commonwealth which led to the emigration of well over a million people from the Afro-Asian world to the United Kingdom were based on a thorough rejection of Hitler's racist ideals. To reject the right of blacks or Asians to live in Britain or the right of American blacks to have equal rights with their fellow citizens was, in a sense, to accept Hitler's racial thesis, a view which no self-respecting person after the Second World War would have anything to do with. Therefore, Hitler's influence, if only in the rejection of his point of view, is still strong today.

Another basic principle of the Nazi regime was the acceptance of war as an instrument of national policy. The tens of millions of people who died as a result of the Second World War, as well as the advent of atomic weapons which use bombs such as the one employed at Hiroshima merely as a trigger to light their fuses, made it quite clear to peoples throughout the world that war as an instrument of national policy was tantamount to national suicide. There have been no large-scale wars since 1945; only wars of a localized nature. No atomic weapons have been employed. Only wars of 'national liberation,' such as the conflicts in Algeria or

Above: Hitler receives the acclamations of the crowd on the tenth anniversary of his coup in Munich on 9 November 1923.

Vietnam, for example, were considered 'legitimate' by world public opinion. This too was a rejection of a Hitlerian principle.

A third principle espoused by Hitler was the right of any nation to aggrandize its power at the expense of other nations. The wave of anti-imperialism which has swept the world since 1945 bears testimony to the rejection of this ideal by world public opinion. It is only justified, as in the case of Cuba's intervention in Angola and the Horn of Africa as a means of helping to rid another country of an 'imperialist' overlord. The argument tends to wear a bit thin when the alleged imperialism of one nation is replaced by that of another, as in the case of Soviet Russia's domination of Poland, Czechoslovakia and other nations of Eastern Europe. Even the Soviet Union, undoubtedly the most successful

Bottom left: Brown House in Munich, headquarters of the National Socialist German Workers' Party.
Below: Naval troops stand at attention as Hitler's car passes after he became Führer and Chancellor of Germany in 1933.

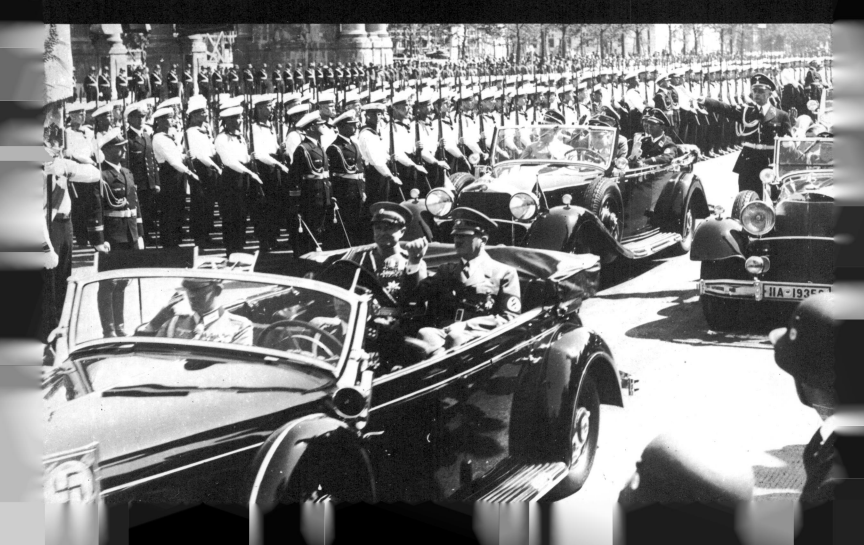

The Leibstandarte Adolf Hitler, the personal bodyguard formed from the elite of the notorious SS, goosestep past Hitler on the Führer's birthday, 20 April 1938.

imperialist aggrandizer since 1945, denies that it is exercising its power at the expense of local nationalism. Russia claims to be the chief anti-imperialist state of all. Outright conquest of one country by another, therefore, has become unfashionable, and this is largely due to Hitler's brutal conquests which totally disregarded the wishes of those whose territories were overrun by Nazi troops.

The fact that Hitler gained such enormous support in Germany throughout the war and the years leading to it, as well as the fact that millions of Europeans who were not German flocked to his racist banner, is a subject of continual fascination for those of us who look back to the 1930s and 1940s and ask the question, 'How could it happen?' The complex personality of Hitler and the effect he had on a a generation are examined in this first, large-format, illustra-

ted biography of Der Führer. Its relevance for readers today lies in the fact that there are still those, especially among younger people, who admire Hitler and who hope to emulate his works. For older readers this book is a reminder of what happened so that it may never recur. Everyone alive today reacts to a greater or lesser extent to what Hitler said and did; *Der Führer: His Life and Times* is the story of one man who dominated a generation and whose influence is still felt. To paraphrase a remark made of Napoleon in the 19th century which can equally apply to Hitler in the 20th century, 'We still live in the shadow of the little corporal.'

Below: Hitler enters the Nuremberg arena for a rally, followed by Bormann, Hess, Himmler, and his aide, Brückner.
Right: A portrait of Der Führer.

Above: Klara Hitler, mother of Adolf Hitler.

Above: The first picture of Hitler, taken in his first year.

The Early Years

Hitler's birth and background have always been open to question. Nevertheless, the rumor, circulated during the war, that he was illegitimate, is quite untrue. Schiklgruber was a family name two generations before, and although his forebears were illegitimate, he was not. His birth was announced in the newspaper (see cuttings right) and he had, by all accounts, a normal childhood and was loved by both parents. His education was equally unremarkable. There is nothing in the man's early life which would give any hint of the sort of man he was to become.

Above: Two announcements of Adolf's birth in local newspapers. A third is shown above his baby picture.

The house in which Hitler was born

Below left, as it appeared during the Nazi period as a national shrine; *below right*, the shabby, lower middle-class origins of Hitler vividly appear at the rear of the residence; *below center*, the rude courtyard in the heart of the apartment block.

Above: Class photograph of the fourth grade at Leonding School. Hitler is in the top row, the fourth child from the left.
Left: Two report cards for Hitler. He was seldom absent and a good student, straight A's during the term shown.
Top right: Hitler's classroom at Fischlham.
Center right: Hitler's second-grade classroom as a national shrine in later years. Note his picture hung just below the cross.
Right: The secondary school in Linz which Hitler attended.

Above: An early sketch drawn by Hitler in 1900 when he was 11 years old and living in Linz, Austria.
Above right: A geometric drawing done by Hitler at Linz.
Right: When Hitler's mother went to hospital in Linz in February 1907, her son paid the bill. This is the hospital register showing his payment of 100 crowns.
Below: Document drawn up at Linz in 1938 certifying the circumstances of Hitler's mother's death when rumors arose that he killed her. The document, ironically, is signed by Dr Eduard Bloch, a Jew.
Hitler's early life was dredged up and analyzed by
the Nazis in excruciating detail after they seized power in order to
enhance the Führer cult they fostered.

The grave of Hitler's parents, festooned
with wreaths donated by the SA.

Hitler im Felde

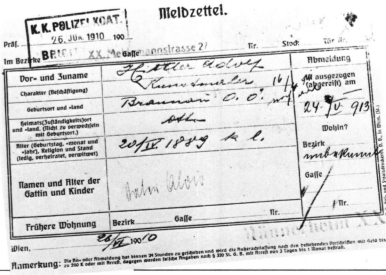

Left and above: A face in the crowd; Hitler cheering the news of the outbreak of World War I.
Above: Hitler's drawing of the Maria Church in Vienna during his years as an artist there before World War I. His style apparently improved over the years.
Bottom far left: Hitler in his German uniform in northern France in 1915. Corporal Hitler sits on the far right.
Bottom center: Another early Hitler drawing done before the war.
Bottom left: Document certifying Hitler's official presence in Vienna in 1913.

Top left: One of Hitler's last prewar sketches of a street in Vienna.
Left: Hitler and fellow German soldiers in a dugout on the Western Front in 1916. Hitler wears the helmet.
Above: Hitler at a field hospital recovering from gassing in 1916. Hitler is on the top row, second from right without a cap.
Right: Army registration of Hitler's disability through gas poisoning.

Above: Hitler at the founding of the Nazi Party in Salzburg in 1920; he sits in the third row above the X.

Above: Hitler and his staff in 1923. From left to right, Maurice, Hitler, Graf, Wagner, Buch and Julius Weber.

Above: Party headquarters on the Corneliusstrasse in Munich in November 1921.

Above: Hitler's Nazi Party card. Note the date of his joining in 1920 and his card number 5.

The Years of Struggle

Below: Hitler in Munich in 1923, with the party 'philosopher' Alfred Rosenberg to the left.

Above left: Hitler in Nuremberg in September 1923. Note the uniform
of the German East African regiment behind him.
Above right: A gathering of the SA in Munich in 1923 at the time of the Beer Hall Putsch.

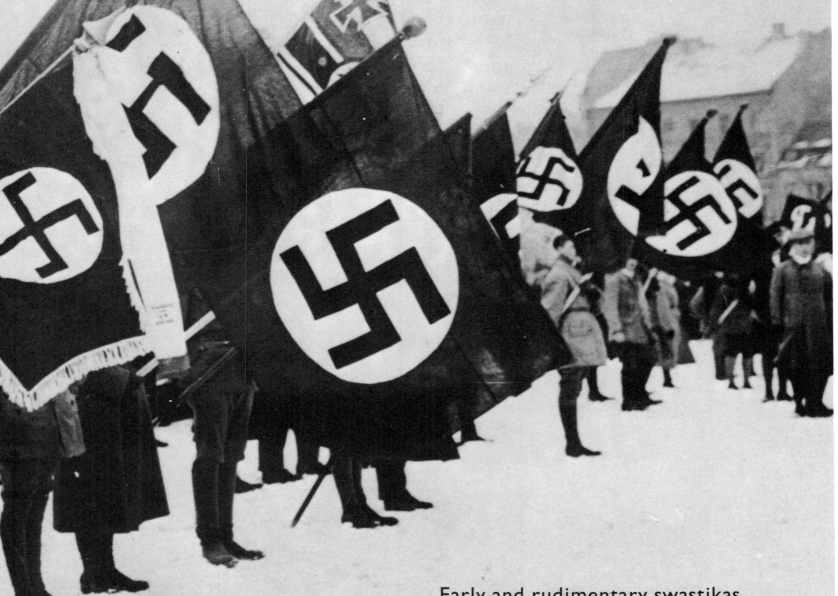

Early and rudimentary swastikas
unfurled at the Champs de Mars in
Munich in January 1923.

PERNET   Dr. WEBER   FRICK   KRIEBEL   LUDENDORFF   HITLER BRÜCKNER   RÖHM   WAGNER

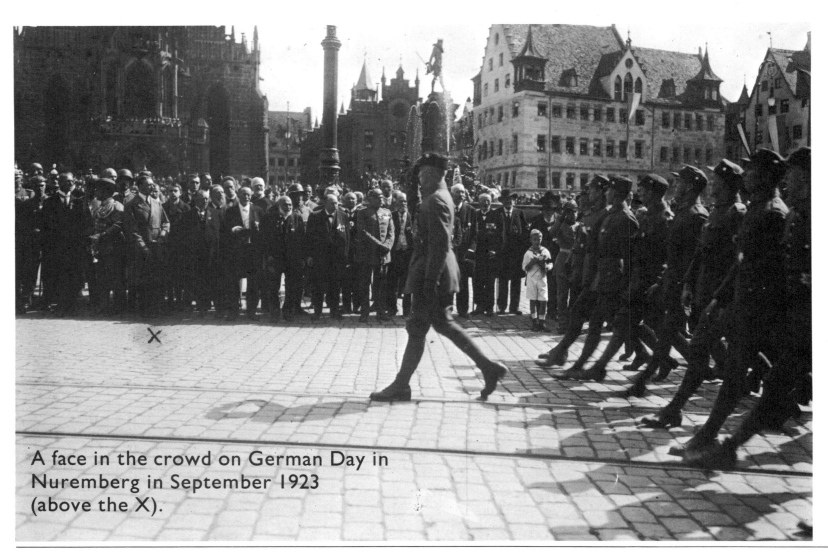

A face in the crowd on German Day in
Nuremberg in September 1923
(above the X).

EXC. v LUDENDORFF   ADOLF HITLER

Left: Hitler, Ludendorff and the other conspirators in the 1923 Munich Beer Hall Putsch.
Above: Ludendorff and Hitler on German Day in the run-up to the November Putsch.
Below: Ludendorff shown a bit too close to Hitler in a faked photograph imposed in 1923. There were sufficient real ones to choose from and this need not have been faked.

Above: Some early banners of the SA used in the 1923 Putsch.

The Beer Hall Putsch

Hitler's attempted coup in Munich which was meant to be a precursor to a German revolution came some months too late. In Hitler's zeal to commemorate the fall of the Kaiser on 9 November 1918 by a coup in Munich in 1923 on the same date, he neglected the fact that the economic crisis which grossly inflated Germany's currency was already halted by foreign loans like the Dawes Plan and the issuance of the Rentenmark, which replaced the almost valueless Reichsmarks. The coup was stopped in its tracks and Hitler was imprisoned.

Hitler in Prison

Hitler served nine months in prison as a result of his complicity in the ill-fated Beer Hall Putsch. It was in Landsberg that he wrote *Mein Kampf*, which was to become the bible of Nazism. Hitler's plan for conquest in Europe and the elimination of the Jews are clearly outlined in this often unreadable document which was dictated to Rudolf Hess. His light sentence for what the Weimar Republic should have considered to have been treason gave the Nazi leader a new role as martyred hero which Hitler made the most of in subsequent years.

Above: Hitler's trial. The chairman of the court Neidhardt appears under (1), Hitler under (2), First Lieutenant Pernet (3) and former Police President of Munich Poehner (4).
Right: Hitler in Landsberg Prison.
Extreme right: The garden and wall of Landsberg.
Extreme right inset: Document sentencing Hitler to Landsberg.

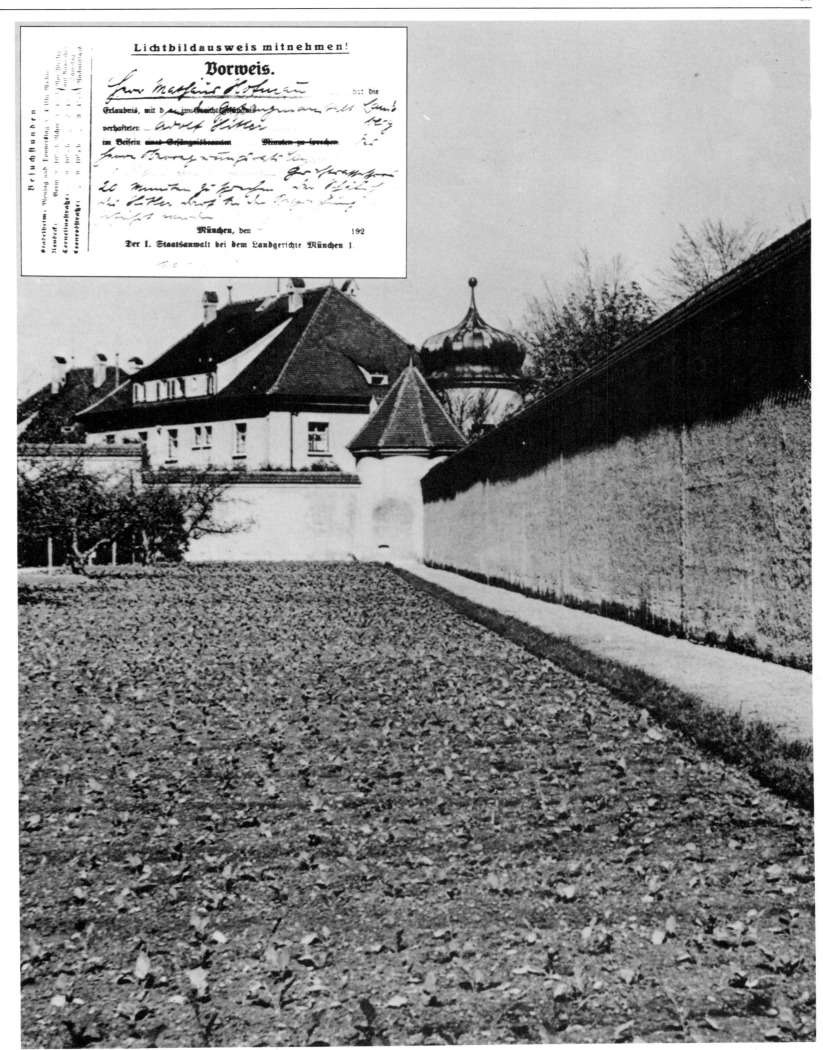

Lichtbildausweis mitnehmen!

Vorweis.

Herr Matthias Hofmann ... hat die

Erlaubnis, mit d ... im Gerichtsgefängnis an ... Land ...

verhafteten: Adolf Hitler ...

im Beisein eines Gefängnisbeamten ... Minuten zu sprechen.

München, den 192

Der I. Staatsanwalt bei dem Landgerichte München I.

Besuchstunden

Stadelheim, Montag und Donnerstag 4 Uhr Nachm.
Neudeck,
Cornelilusstraße,
Leonrodstraße,

Left: Hitler on his release from Landsberg.
Above: A Nazi Party newspaper celebrates Hitler's release.
Below: Hitler leaves Landsberg Prison in December 1924.
Right: Hitler visits Landsberg ten years after his release.

Left: A poster announces Hitler's speech at the Bürgerbräukeller in Munich where the 1923 Putsch was held. The subject was 'Germany's Future and Our Movement.'
Above: Hitler leaves Brown House in Munich, by now the Party headquarters.
Below: Inside Brown House where the Nazi Party files were kept under lock and key.
Right: A Nazi sympathizer being led away by a policeman after a demonstration.

Years of Recovery

After the failure of the Beer Hall Putsch and Hitler's imprisonment the Nazi Party went into a decline. As Germany's economic situation improved the party faced some lean years.

Above: Hitler greets a man wounded in a street fight against the Communists.
Below: Hitler visits a wounded SA man in hospital.

The Early Rallies

As enthusiasm began to grow for the Nazis once more, pressure on the government increased to ban the rallies and stem the Nazi tide.

Right: SA men line up shirtless when uniforms were temporarily banned.
Below: Hitler greets SA leaders in 1927 at a rally.
Below right: Potatoes are peeled to feed SA men at the rally.
Bottom: SA men cheer their Führer when he appeared to address them.
Opposite top: An early SA rally in 1922.
Opposite bottom: Hitler Youth and SA personnel greet Hitler's arrival in a small Bavarian village.

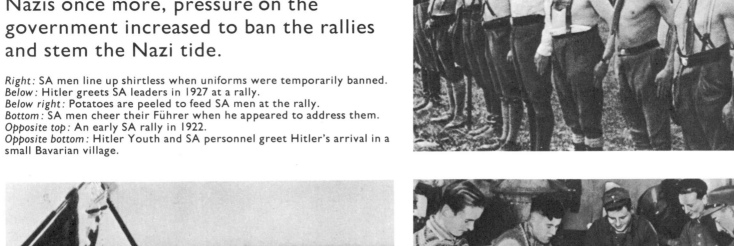

Above: Hitler studies his notes before a small meeting of SA men. Note Rudolf Hess on the left. Hess was an early supporter of Hitler and remained his second-in-command until 1941.

Above: Hitler with Gregor Strasser (left) in Bavaria in 1927. Strasser was Hitler's chief rival for party leadership, who was brushed aside and subsequently assassinated in 1934.

Above: Reichs Party Day in Nuremberg in 1927. Hitler salutes parading SA men with his new recruit, Paul Josef Goebbels, on the left.
Left: Hitler in the Bavarian woods. Hitler's love for Bavaria continued after his seizure of power, and many weeks of the year were spent in Hitler's mountain retreat in Berchtesgaden.

Above: Hitler and Goebbels (right) in 1926 shortly after the future propaganda minister pledged his support. He had previously backed the left-wing of the party led by the Strasser brothers.
Right: A 1927 photograph with Hitler wearing his ubiquitous Iron Cross, won in World War I.

Above: Hitler grasps the bloody flag of the 1923 Putsch, a symbol of martyrdom, at Reichs Party Day at Nuremberg in 1929.
Right: Hitler and Julius Streicher, the vituperative anti-Semite, at Party Day in Nuremberg in 1927.
Far right: Himmler, Hess, Gregor Strasser, Hitler and Pfeffer von Salomon in Nuremberg in 1927.

Above: A new Nazi group is formed in Thuringia in 1929. *Below*: Hitler salutes the SA at a rally in Weimar in 1930.

Above: Party Day in Nuremberg, 19–20 August 1927. From the left Georg Halberman, Pfeffer von Salomon, Hess and Hitler salute the parade of SA troops.

Top left: Hitler and his staff in Braunschweig in February 1931.
Top center: Hitler and Manfred von Killinger, Reichs commissar for Saxony in 1932.
Top right: Von Killinger greets Hess and Hitler at party headquarters in Saxony.
Below: Hess, Himmler, Röhm and Frick with their Führer in Gera in September 1931.

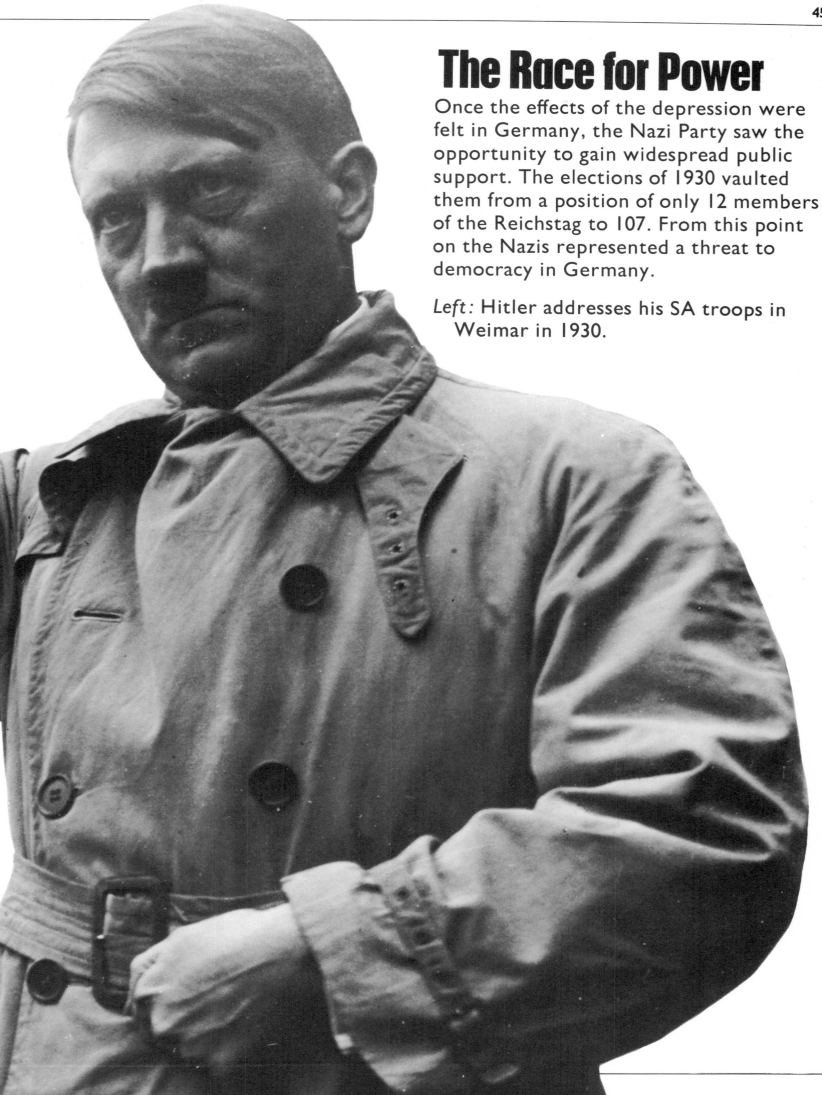

The Race for Power

Once the effects of the depression were felt in Germany, the Nazi Party saw the opportunity to gain widespread public support. The elections of 1930 vaulted them from a position of only 12 members of the Reichstag to 107. From this point on the Nazis represented a threat to democracy in Germany.

Left: Hitler addresses his SA troops in Weimar in 1930.

Above: Storm troopers march past Hitler at Braunschweig in 1931.
Far left: Hitler working in his study at Dachenfeld House.
Left: Hitler with Julius Schreck, a later martyr of the Nazi Party.
Right: Hitler with members of the Reichs Führer School, which trained SA leaders, in 1932.

Above: National Party leader Hugenberg, later a subject of a homosexual scandal, with Prince Eitel Friedrich.
Below: A faked picture showing Hitler to the Prince's right, meant to damage Hitler's reputation. It did not.

Above: A portrait taken at Berchtesgaden in 1932. From left to right, Gregor Strasser, Röhm, Hitler, Goering and Bruckner. After he took power Hitler had the first two assassinated in the Blood Purge of 1934.
Below: Hitler at a meeting in the cellar of Brown House in Munich, the party headquarters, in 1930.
Above right: A Nazi meeting at the Bürgerbräukeller in 1929 or there-abouts, the Munich beer hall where the 1923 putsch began.
Below right: Gregor Strasser (left of Hitler) and Dr Frick at a meeting deciding Strasser's fate as an important party leader. His fate was sealed in the mid-1920s when Hitler gained full control of the party and turned the Nazis into supporting capitalist and other right-wing interests at the expense of the party's erstwhile socialist ideals. Robert Ley, Alfred Rosenberg and Ritter von Epp appear near the foreground.

Above: Hitler lays down the law to a party meeting at the Hotel Kaiserhof in Berlin in 1932. Goering and Frick are to Hitler's left; Goebbels, Frank and Brückner in the background right.

Paul Josef Goebbels

Goebbels was a critical and valuable addition to Hitler's entourage. Not only was he a great orator, arguably more persuasive than Hitler, but he brought the support of the left-wing, socialist-oriented Nazis behind Hitler's leadership.

Left: Goebbels greets Hitler before a speech.
Below: Goebbels in a pensive mood prior to a major speech at the Sportpalast.

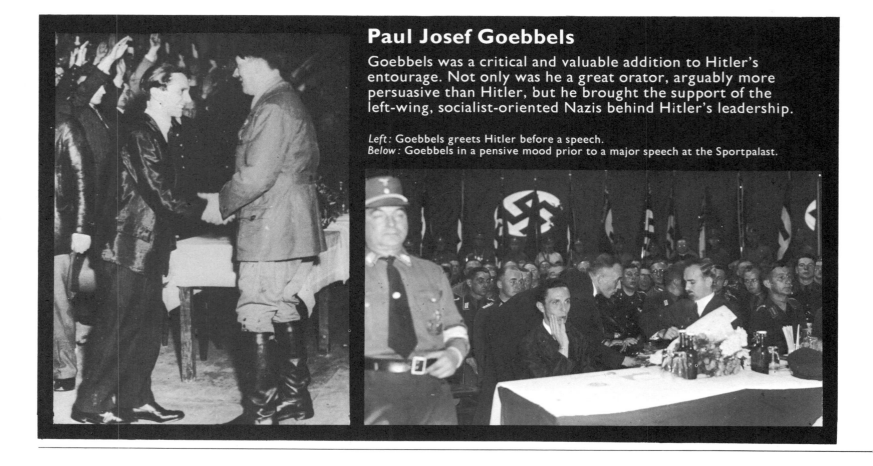

Above: Goebbels addresses a gathering of the SA in a Berlin street in 1931. He was made party leader in the capital to whip up support for the Nazis in the traditionally left-wing city.

Above: A subtle message to residents and visitors of the Hotel Adlon, the social center of Berlin, whose bar was frequented by the wealthy and famous of German café society.

Above: Over 200,000 massed in the Lustgarten of Berlin to protest the 'shame of Versailles.' Part of the Nazi appeal was based on bitter hatred of the politicians who had dishonored Germany by signing the *Diktat*.

Above: An anti-Hitler slogan is daubed next to a Berlin canal. Often these slogans were erased or defaced by young Nazis after they were drawn.

Above: SA members in Mecklenburg try to convince their neighbors to vote for Hitler in 1932.

Above: Wall posters in a Berlin working class area support the Nazis in the election of 1930.

Above: Nazi leaders von Ulrich, Heines, Himmler, General Ritter von Epp, SA Leader Röhm, and Count Helldorf, later to become Berlin police chief.
Below: Hitler appeals to the student vote in a speech given at the University of Berlin in 1931.

Above: Hitler attends the wedding dinner of Schaub. He made it a point to attend all weddings of longtime Nazi leaders.

Above: Hitler gives a speech in Berlin's Lustgarten that was also broadcast on radio throughout Germany. The Führer used the radio more effectively than any contemporary political leader, and was one of the first to recognize its importance.
Below: The audience listening to that speech. Older people in the audience were professors or university workers.

Above: Hitler at a youth meeting in 1932 in Potsdam. Hitler Youth Leader Baldur von Schirach stands to Hitler's right.
Left: Hitler and Goering at Tempelhof airfield in Berlin in November 1932.
Below: Hitler accepts flowers from a child with SS Leader Sepp Dietrich on the left and Magda Goebbels on Hitler's right; this picture was taken minutes after the one on the left.

Above: Von Helldorf, Hitler, Engel, Goebbels and Brückner (Hitler's personal adjutant) at a well-attended political demonstration in Berlin's Sportpalast in 1932.
Below left: Hitler with flowers (presented in left picture) and Goering at Tempelhof with SS guards.
Below right: Hitler, Goering and Röhm a few minutes later.
Bottom right: Hitler and Julius Schreck in Berlin. Hitler wore a black armband in homage to Horst Wessel, a martyred hero of the Hitler Youth.

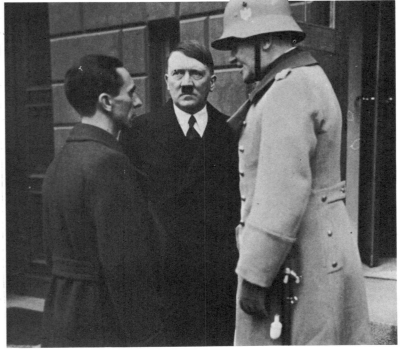

Far left top: SA Leader Maikowski (right) congratulates police chief Zauritz for his suppression of Communist demonstrations in Berlin.
Center left top: Goebbels, Hitler and Wehrmacht Chief of Staff von Blomberg (later purged) at a moment when Hitler was currying favor with the military before he seized power.
Left: Hitler and SA Chief Röhm at Party Day in Nuremberg in 1933 as thousands of SA men stand at attention. This was the last such occasion for Röhm, who was executed by the Nazis in the Night of the Long Knives on 30 June 1934.
Below: Hitler and Goebbels visit the grave of Horst Wessel, whose song became a second German national anthem after the seizure of power.

The Seizure of Power

On 30 January 1933 Hitler was summoned by President Hindenburg to become Chancellor of Germany. It was thought at the time that with only three Nazis in the Cabinet, and Vice-Chancellor von Papen to control Hitler, taking a chance in nominating the leader of the party with a plurality in the Reichstag was worth the risk. It was thought that once Hitler was in power, he would be constrained and unable to exercise his more extreme policies. But within six months Hitler and the Nazi Party controlled every organ of state and society except one, the armed forces.

Far left: Hitler's car returns to the Wilhelmstrasse after he was made Chancellor.
Bottom far left: Hitler's first photograph as Chancellor.
Left: Hitler arrives at the Hotel Kaiserhof for a victory celebration.
Center left: Nazi Party leaders the day Hitler became Chancellor. From left to right: Kube, Kerrl (seated), Frick, Goebbels, Hitler, Röhm, Goering, Darré, Himmler and Hess.
Bottom left: Hitler acknowledges cheers from supporters at the Wilhelmstrasse on the night of victory after the torchlight parade.
Below: The Nazi Party newspaper announces the news of the seizure of power the following day.
Bottom: Hitler and Goering wave to the thousands outside the Reichschancellery.

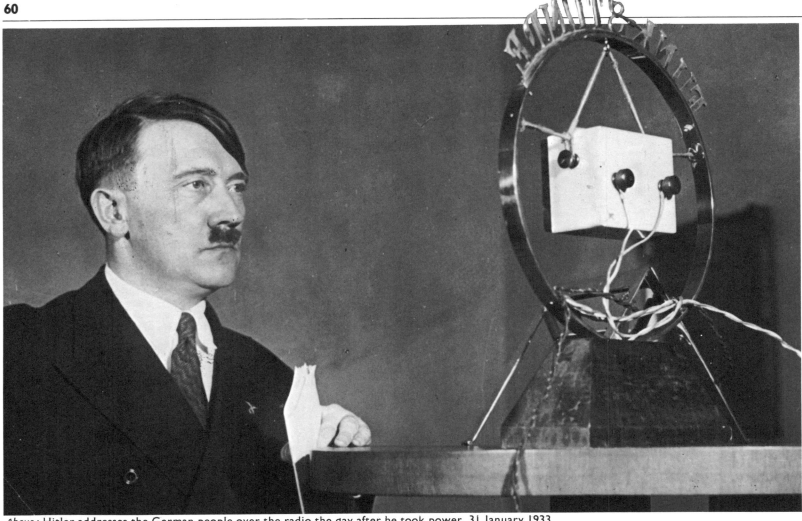

Above: Hitler addresses the German people over the radio the day after he took power, 31 January 1933.
Below: Election day in 1933, the last free elections held in Germany until after 1945. The Nazis won.

Above: Hitler addresses the crowd at the Sportpalast in Berlin in March 1933 prior to the election.

Above: Berlin police carry the Nazi banners in the campaign of 1933.
Below: Hitler addresses President Hindenburg in Potsdam, 21 March 1933.

Above: An homageful Hitler speaks to Crown Prince Wilhelm, the ex-Kaiser's son, in front of Potsdam's Garrison Church.

Hitler and Hindenburg

Field Marshal Otto von Hindenburg was Germany's most celebrated hero of World War I. He was elected President of Germany after the death of Friedrich Ebert in 1925, and ran again in 1932 while in his eighties against Hitler. He won, but grudgingly accepted Hitler as his Chancellor in January 1933. Before he died on 2 August 1934, Hitler used the great reputation of this now senile and feeble old man to enhance his own legitimacy. After Hindenburg's death, Hitler forged the Field Marshal's Political Testament to make it appear as if Hindenburg wanted Hitler to succeed him, a prospect which the old gentleman feared. Immediately after his death Hitler merged the offices of Chancellor and President into one, Der Führer. The leader of the Nazi Party had finally become the sole leader of the German nation.

Top left: Hitler meets Hindenburg at the Garrison Church in Potsdam on 21 March 1933 under the watchful eye of General von Blomberg.
Left: President and Chancellor arrive in Berlin's Lustgarten on 1 May 1933.
Above: Hitler bows to his President at the State Opera House in Berlin in 1934 as Oskar von Hindenburg watches.
Right: Hitler and Hindenburg at the Tannenberg Memorial, commemorating the battle site of Hindenburg's greatest victory.

Rallies

Hitler and Goebbels staged massive rallies involving often over 100,000 people at a time at every conceivable occasion. In addition to the annual rallies held at Nuremberg until the outbreak of war, others honoring various armed services as well as the paramilitary organizations, the SA and SS, were opportunities to flaunt Germany's military strength, both real and imaginary, to Hitler's potential enemies. They were equally an opportunity to impress the solidarity of public support for the Nazi Party on foreigners as well as on those Germans who were opposed to the regime. Broadcast on radio throughout Germany and subsequently all over Europe and America, they frightened enemies of Germany and encouraged her supporters and fellow travelers. They were a vital part of the consolidation of support for the Third Reich.

Above: Krause drives and Kempka and Ley discuss the occasion as Hitler arrives in Nuremberg for Party Day, 1937.

Below: The Navy marches past its Führer on Party Day in Nuremberg, in the autumn of 1935.

Above: Hitler reviews the SS on Party Day, 1937. By this time the SS was the most feared and powerful organization in Germany. It had its own schools, housing settlements, hospitals and so on. Its obedience to Hitler was total and its administration of security ruthless.
Below: Hitler and Baldur von Schirach, head of the Hitler Youth, 1934.

Hitler with the bloody flag of the Beer Hall Putsch of November 1923 which became a totem for Nazi rallies during the formative Weimar and Nazi years.

Above: German girls wait at a window to watch their Führer pass by.
Below: SA troops mass for a rally in Dresden in 1932.

Above: The *Avantguardia*, Mussolini's fascist vanguard, visit Brown House in Munich in 1932.

Walters kampf für Hitler

Von Hermann Schauff

Above: The soldiers of the SA march through Munich in 1932.
Below: German workers march in support of Hitler in 1932.

Above: 'Walter's struggle for Hitler,' a propaganda book issued to recruits of the Hitler Youth.

Hitler addresses an SA rally in Dortmund in 1933.

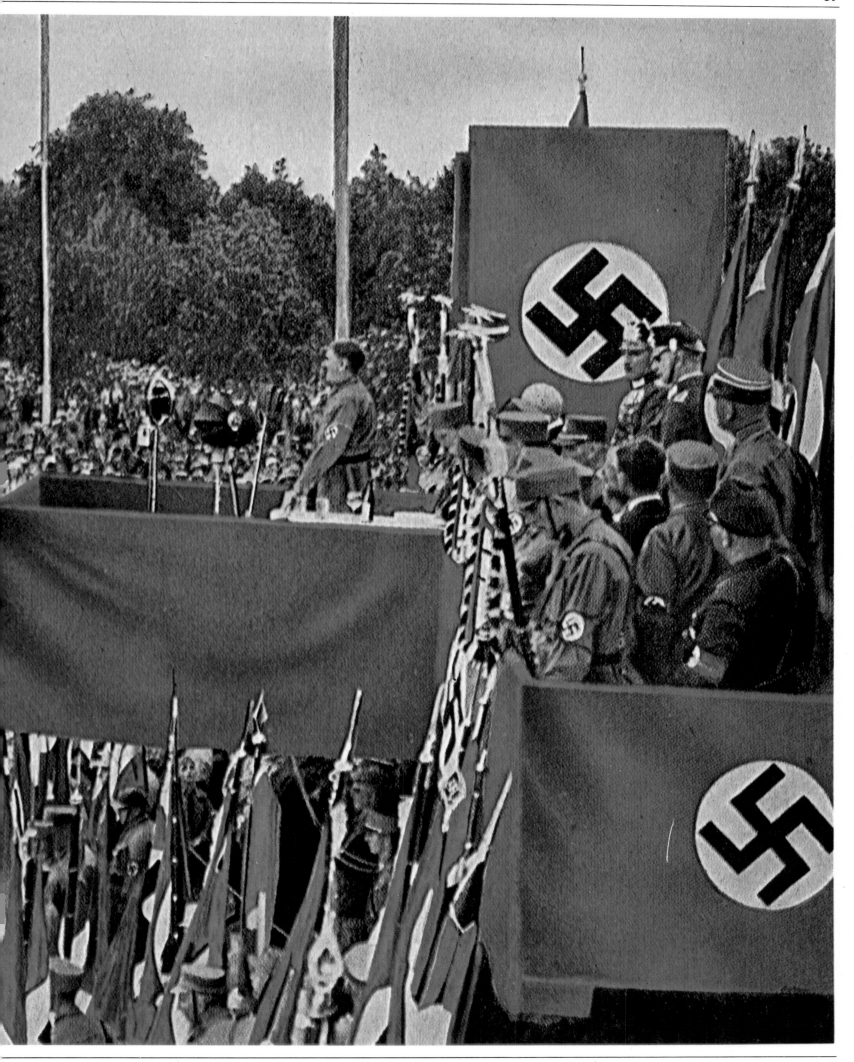

Dedication and launching of the cruiser *Admiral Scheer* in 1933.

Above: Hitler Youth parade before their leader, Baldur von Schirach, in Nuremberg in 1933. Julius Streicher stands to his left.
Below: Goebbels (right) salutes the parade of the German Turnfest in Stuttgart in 1933.

Above: Hitler arrives at the Hotel Deutscher Hof in Nuremberg on Party Day.
Below: Himmler, Lütze and Hitler and a cast of thousands on Party Day, 1934.

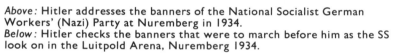

Above: Hitler addresses the banners of the National Socialist German Workers' (Nazi) Party at Nuremberg in 1934.
Below: Hitler checks the banners that were to march before him as the SS look on in the Luitpold Arena, Nuremberg 1934.

Above: Goering and Hitler confer on Party Day, 1933.
Right: Workers carrying their spades like rifles march through Nuremberg on their way to the rally.
Below: Antiquated light tanks parade past the Führer on Party Day, 1934.

Below: Hitler delivers his speech to 60,000 Hitler Youths on Party Day, 1934. Baldur von Schirach stands in the background.

Above: Hitler salutes members of the Labor Corps on Party Day, 1933.
Below: Hitler addresses the Hitler Youth on Party Day, 1934. These rallies were held often before the war.

Below: Hitler and Hess at the opening of the Luitpold Arena in Nuremberg in 1933. This arena was the scene of the largest Nazi rallies.

Above: Frick and Hess stand by as members of the Labor Front march past
Below: Leni Riefenstahl, who made two classic films in praise of the Reich,
Triumph of the Will and *Olympiad*, at Party Day in 1935.

Below: Von Blomberg, Goering, Fritsch and Hitler on Party Day, 1935.
The two generals were purged in 1938, leaving Hitler largely in control
of the Wehrmacht.

Above: Hitler checks seating and standing arrangements on the Nuremberg arena.
Below: Hitler chats with workers preparing for the Nuremberg rally.

Below: Hitler makes an irregular and spontaneous appearance at the window of his suite in the Hotel Deutscher Hof in the rally town of Nuremberg on Party Day.

Below: Hitler and Speer check the construction work on the arena in Nuremberg.

Above: Hess, Hitler, Speer, Streicher, Wagner and Schwarz before a speech on Party Day.
Below: Von Schirach and the Führer pass through the ranks of Hitler Youth.

Below: Hitler addresses a spectacular crowd of over 100,000 on Party Day, 1935. It was in 1935 that Hitler officially rejected the Treaty of Versailles and openly began to rearm Germany.

Goebbels in Power

Paul Josef Goebbels was the greatest propagandist the world has ever known. Once he attained power as Hitler's propaganda minister, the entire force and power of the Reich were at his disposal. His aim was to destroy the fabric of traditional Germany and replace it with groups and organizations purged of any opposition to the regime. To accomplish these ends, posters, rallies, radio broadcasts and films were mobilized. Goebbels had an open brief from Hitler because of the propagandist's total loyalty to the Führer, whom he worshipped. Of all Hitler's lieutenants Goebbels was the most loyal. He was probably also the most effective and brilliant of them as well.

Above: Dr Goebbels upon receiving his new office as Minister of Propaganda.
Below: Goebbels was party leader in Berlin before the seizure of power and whipped up support for the Nazis throughout the capital.

Above: Goebbels opens a youth rally in Berlin's Lustgarten in May 1933.
Below: Goebbels and his aide, State Secretary Hanke.
Right: Goebbels and Hitler in 1938 read the text of a speech.

Propaganda

"The most brilliant propaganda technique must confine itself to a few points and repeat them over and over." *Adolf Hitler*

Right: The lights remain on at a Hamburg store.
Far right: Poster for an exhibition of 'approved' art in Munich, 1937.
Center right: Postcard commemorating three German leaders: Frederick the Great, Bismarck and Hitler.

Above: One People, One Reich, One Führer is the theme of this famous poster.

ENTARTETE KUNST

AUSSTELLUNG DER NSDAP
IM HAUS DER KUNST AM KÖNIGSPLATZ

KARTEN ZU ERMÄSSIGTEN HIER
VORVERKAUFSPREISEN

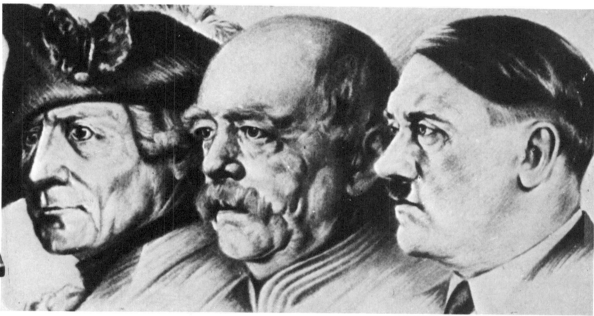

efiehl, wir folgen!
sagen Ja!

Above: Hitler Youth promote the
cause in 1934. The slogan says, 'The
Führer Orders; We Follow.'
Right: A rural family listens to a
Hitler speech on the radio.

Hitler as Traditionalist

While appealing to the conservative instincts of most Germans, Hitler's Reich demolished or mortally weakened the fabric of traditional Germany. In order to create his new order, Hitler took every opportunity to create harmless links with the past at the moment he was erasing the centuries-old traditions which were Germany. Meetings such as this one, with 85-year-old General Litzmann, endeared Hitler to his people and supported the myth that he was preserving German culture, not destroying it.

Right: Hitler greets Litzmann on his arrival on the Lüneberg Heath for the maneuvers of 1935.
Below right: Hitler congratulates Karl Litzmann on his 85th birthday.
Below: Hitler greets the old general once again in his car.
Far right: The Führer escorts the old gentleman through the SS honor guard.

Consolidation of Power

The first six months of Hitler's regime were the most revolutionary in the history of Germany. In every town and village, institutions from boys' clubs to women's groups, card and chess playing societies as well as sports organizations were eliminated. In place of perhaps dozens of such groups in every fair-sized town, one government or party-led organization replaced them. All boys' clubs were incorporated into the Hitler Youth. Women's clubs were amalgamated into the League of German Women (BdM). Sports groups became part of the Strength Through Joy (KdF) movement. This period called *Gleichschaltung* is difficult to translate. In principle it meant the equalization or re-organization of society, weaving one Nazi fabric of the hundreds of strands which are the consistency of any civilized society. On 1 May 1933 a rally was held in Berlin to celebrate this subordination of individual will to the will of the Party, which was fast becoming the State.

Left: Poster above Hitler's head says 'The Youth greets the Workers and the Führer.'
Below: Vice-Chancellor von Papen, General von Blomberg, Hitler and Goebbels on 1 May 1933 in Berlin.
Right: Hitler arrives at the 1 May celebrations guarded by SS men.

Leibstandarte Adolf Hitler

Hitler created a personal bodyguard, or Leibstandarte, among elite members of the elitist SS. They were carefully chosen among the best physical specimens the SS had to offer, and this unit, originally honorary, became one of Germany's most formidable military units during World War II. The Leibstandarte was more than a paramilitary and later a military unit. It was the physical embodiment of Nazism and fanaticism.

Left: Hitler and the Leibstandarte's commander, Sepp Dietrich, review the troops in 1935.
Below: Hitler salutes the Leibstandarte in front of the Kroll Opera House in Berlin in 1938.

Above: The LAH, as the Leibstandarte (Hitler's personal bodyguard) was called, present arms.

Above: Sepp Dietrich and Hitler inspect the barracks of the LAH.
Below: Himmler and Hitler review the LAH in Nuremberg on Party Day.

The Making of a Tyrant
A British View

The pessimists notwithstanding, human history contains mercifully few monsters. Even among those convicted by earlier ages there has been a tendency of late to hand out free pardons – Nero, for instance, or Nicholas II of Russia. It is hard to realize that this mild little man with his neatly trimmed beard was once regarded as the most hated personnage in both Europe and North America.

Those who have brought a sustained shudder to the human race, or a great part of it, remain a select group – Genghis Khan, Tamburlaine, perhaps Attila the Hun. And it is a chastening thought that our own century has added two indisputable names, those of Josef Vissarionovich Dzhugashvili, alias Stalin and of Adolf Hitler.

There is even danger in listing them thus. As real as Genghis, Attila or Tamburlaine were, as atrocious many of their crimes, dramatization, as for example in Christopher Marlowe's *Tamburlaine the Great,* has at once rendered them blacker and larger than life, and hence diminished their reality for us. Hitler and Stalin are something more than the stuff of splendid melodramas, as the deaths of millions and the wrecked, dwarfed lives of such as survived their malice testify. In any event, they raised organized terror to such heights that other conquerors could never aspire to, if, indeed, they had the ambition to try.

Hitler was born at Braunau-am-Inn, between Austria and Bavaria, at 1830 hours on the evening 20 April 1889. He was not illegitimate so there was never any justification for applying his grandmother's maiden name of Schiklgruber to him. The truth was that his father, Alois Hitler, an Austrian custom's official who had been born out of wedlock to Maria Schiklgruber, subsequently had his birth legitimized. The false aspersion of bastardy was first cast upon him by Viennese

enemies in the 1930s and revived by Allied propaganda. It still enjoys currency.

Adolf was the third child of his father's third marriage, the earlier children both dying in infancy. A brother, Edward, born after him, also died at the age of six and only a sister, Paula, survived. The second of Alois' wives, Franziska Matzelberger (who had died of consumption), had produced two children, Alois and Angela. As a widow, Angela was to become her half brother's housekeeper at Berchtesgaden and it was with her daughter, Angelika 'Geli' Raubal that Hitler was to pursue a strange and – for her – tragic love affair.

The family milieu was rural and modest in the extreme. Alois' father had been a miller; he himself had been apprenticed to a cobbler. His appointment to what was, however insignificant a post in the Civil Service of the Austro-Hungarian Empire, represented no small achievement, therefore, especially to one who had begun life under the stigma of illegitimacy.

We know he took his advancement in station seriously, regarding his uniform as the very emblem of imperial authority, insisting on the use of his proper title, and conducting himself 'strictly . . . even pedantically' in the words of a Custom House colleague. This is in strange contrast with the violent, drink besotted brute whom, according to later legend, the child Hitler had to lead home from 'smoky taverns' in the early hours. One is forced to dismiss the legend if only because throughout his life Hitler showed himself the product of a cautious, self-consciously respectable and conservative upbringing. Even his prejudices were those of the lower middle class: anti-Semitism, for example; or hostility to the upper classes, who by mere right of birth barred the way to others; or suspicion and fear of a coarse, potentially rebellious proletariat.

The Hitler myth, skillfully embellished by Goebbels and fostered by the Führer himself, presented the boy as an instinc-

Below: Some early supporters of Hitler in Munich prior to the Beer Hall Putsch of 8–9 November 1923.

Above: The pro-Nazi cell in Coburg in 1922. Note the rude formation of the swastika armbands.

tive leader whom his play fellows unquestioningly followed. At 11 he 'understood the meaning of history,' a precocious achievement which set him above his fellow countryman Mozart who at that age had, after all, merely produced a few symphonies and had not even tried to solve the problem which had vexed philosophy from its inception.

At school there is every reason to suppose he was bright and intelligent, but his academic career was marred by his congenital inability to sustain any effort, a characteristic which dogged him through life and aroused comment from most of those who came into lengthy contact with him. Albert Speer, to take one from a host of witnesses, mentions the difficulty his aides had in persuading him to prepare his great 'Cultural Speeches' for the Nuremberg Rallies. Invariably they had to be completed on the eve of their delivery.

There is a vital clue to much in the nature of the Third Reich in this, particularly that questing aggressiveness which impelled it from one perilous adventure to the next, often before the destiny of the first had been put beyond hazard.

Remembering the nation's acts were at this time precisely those of its leader, one asks oneself what the cause was? The main suspect must be conflict between father and son. The older man, probably finicky and exacting, too ready to find fault with the younger; the son retaliating by looking upon his father as a dull, unadventurous drudge. There is no doubt that Hitler hated his father – he could not otherwise have brought himself to calumny him, even in self-justification. Such hatred is in large part projected self-hatred. The accusations of father against son, coming *de haut en bas*, are always in some measure accepted, to be reinforced by life's routine failures which look

like the father's admonitions vindicated. The result is a deep-seated guilt complex and escape through the progressive abandonment of reality in favor of fantasy.

Through its beguiling images the dreamer becomes master in one field, then another, gathering his reward of adulation, fame and wealth. It is all the better when he alights on some sphere quite outside the general experience of his associates, for then none can question him. So in provincial Linz, to which the family moved after the death of Alois in 1903, Hitler, no doubt on the small encouragement of some kindly teacher, conceived the idea that his destiny lay in art.

As is typical of the inveterate fantasist, who knows reality to be littered with pitfalls and discouragements, Hitler appears not to have taken a single practical step towards the achievement of his dream. Of the great movements in art in the Austria of that time, which was in such exciting ferment, or of the ideas behind them, he knew nothing and took no pains to inform himself.

This need hardly surprise us, for the truth is that what differentiates the real artist from his neurotic imitator is that for the former the act of creation is relished for its own sake, above all else. The appearance of bohemian contempt for convention stems out of this. It is not a uniform put on so that the world knows him for an artist. At the same time success is a mere trapping, even a handicap in that it can hinder his freedom to return to canvas, clay, keyboard or writing desk. There is not a jot of evidence that Hitler was ever urged on by the desire to give physical form to a relentless, internal vision.

The widowed Frau Hitler found the boy quite beyond her control. In view of the tragedies which had overwhelmed her other offspring, she had almost certainly pampered him. From Alfred Adler, for whom this lay at the heart of all neuroses, and who was himself a refugee from the Nazis, we have an illuminating portrait of the pampered child. 'At one time dependent on other people' he writes, 'at another longing to suppress them, such children soon come up against opposition, insurmountable for them, of a world which demands fellowship and cooperation. Robbed of their illusions, they blame other people and always see only a hostile principle in life.' (Alfred Adler, *Social Interest: A Challenge to Mankind*, London, 1938.) Through his life, Hitler never had a single, close friend. He was indeed actively disliked by most of those from whom intimates are drawn: neighbors, school-fellows, workmates, even comrades in the army. Of the two people who came nearest to him, he quarreled with both and had one murdered when he was in a position to do so. One cannot help suspecting, too, that his mother's treatment of the boy was a cause of conflict between the parents, with its attendant damage to his psychological development.

Certainly after one further attempt, by way of a new school, to get him to complete his studies, in 1907 she gave in to his long-nurtured desire to go to Vienna, there to become a famous artist. Supported by his mother and now 18 years old, he made his first attempt at entering the Vienna Academy of Fine Arts. His test drawing was regarded as unsatisfactory and he was rejected. A further assault on the stronghold of Viennese artistic orthodoxy the following year did not even take him through its doors. He was rejected without taking the test on the basis of his preliminary drawings.

Advised to try his hand at architecture instead, he could not even attempt entry to the Academy of Architecture as he had never acquired the certificate to prove satisfactory completion of his school studies.

It had been a disappointing two years made worse by his mother's death in the December of 1908. The great 'ifs' of history are as intriguing as they are vain: this very tragedy actually postponed the cathartic facing of reality for the young Hitler by providing him with an inheritance. This, on top of the proceeds of the sale of the family property, plus a pension as the orphan of a state servant which Hitler drew, quite fraudulently, by pretending to be undergoing full time education, enabled him to live in idle comfort. Though later he was to represent these years as a time of purgative austerity, the 'discipline of the garret' thought essential to all artists, his real income, says his German biographer, Joachim Fest, was about the equivalent of a junior magistrate of the times.

He was able to lounge round the cafés all day; go to the theater or the opera house at night, revelling particularly in Wagner. It was an existence which must, in retrospect, have suited him to the ground. At one moment he would occupy himself writing a play, based like the Wagnerian operas on Germanic legend; at another he even embarked on an opera; at another he declared himself to be involved in some grandiose scheme for the total replanning of Vienna's working class area; at another he would sit doing drawings or water-colors, full of minute, lifeless detail; at another, decide his fortune was to be made as an inventor.

All very immature, but harmless enough – the neurotic needs his hate-object, however; there must, in Adler's words, be 'someone to blame.' Why else should the products of his genius fail to receive their just reward? Hitler found the answer in the endemic anti-Semitism of the times.

The origins of this lay in Russia and Poland where the endless pogroms had forced long-established Jewish populations to move west in search of a more hospitable habitat. Strange beings inured to life in the ghettoes, standing out with beard, skullcap and kaftan, unlike the Europeanized Jews of earlier migrations, their arrival was hailed as a disaster not least of all among their better established co-religionists. In a very short time anti-Semitic feelings were such as to keep them out of the professions, even the senior universities. With this, among the more fanatical anti-Semites, went the invention of nonstrous Jewish plots of world domination and racial pollution. All this the young Hitler absorbed as excitedly as if he had been given the secret of the Cosmos.

United with that perversion of the Theory of Evolution, Social Darwinism, it became an integrated system in his mind. Struggle was the basic law of life; through it the fit survived and the weak perished. Because of the immutable workings of this law the fit had indeed an intrinsic right not merely to survival but to destroy the weak as parasites.

Among the weak, and therefore to be despised, were the Jews. They had survived, however, as vermin – the rat, the louse – had survived. And as Mankind had the right to destroy and if possible exterminate other vermin it also had the right to destroy its human vermin.

Such ideas now startle us by their very crudity and in an era in which the notion of the 'struggle for existence' has given place to one of balance in a world preoccupied with ecology, it is hard to realize how seriously such distortions were taken. It is easy to understand their appeal to a neurotic anxious to offload his own guilt.

Although even Hitler's own accounts give the impression that it was matters of political philosophy that took up most of his time plainly it was not so. But apart from his visits to the opera house and theater or his loitering round cafés we are left to wonder how he filled the hours. Of his sexual proclivities we have little reliable evidence save such as would lead us to suppose his appetites were normal, if not outwardly, excessive. There is the story of his alleged rape of an artist's model while she was posing and another of his contracting syphilis from a Jewish prostitute, the supposed root of his anti-Semitism. That he had venereal disease is possible on the basis of some later evidence, but that infection from a Jewess was the motive for his hatred of her race seems unlikely. And as to the model incident, whatever else, Hitler was plainly too anxious for a reputation for bourgeois respectability to hazard it so openly.

Though perfectly capable of charm and even gallantry, the probability is that there was something repugnant to young girls about this strangely intense youth with his rapid oscillation of mood from gaiety and ceaseless activity to black, lethargic depression. Witnesses are unanimous in describing him as pallid, with watery blue eyes that were capable of blazing with alarming passion when he embarked on some pet hatred, such as that he felt toward the Jews.

It was only when his inheritance was exhausted that the life of doss-houses and men's hostels, of which so much was made later, actually began. Then it was, too, that he took to tricking out his state orphan's pension by working on building sites – though remaining aloof from his workmates – and by producing the little water colors of Vienna which one of his doss-house companions sold for him as he was too proud, too anxious to protect the patina respectability so to demean himself.

In 1913, Vienna having failed him on all counts, he left his native country for the German Reich and took up residence in Munich. He speaks of this as the fulfillment of a longing to tread the earth from which the German people, of which the Austrians were a mere scion, had sprung. As we know, it was actually an attempt to evade his army call up. When it failed and he was picked up by the German police, he sent to the Viennese authorities a rambling, cringing, semi-literate letter of excuse, filled with self-pity and with such details of his personal affairs as can have been of no conceivable interest to those to whom it was addressed. In fact, when at last he did report for his medical examination he was immediately rejected on health grounds.

War and Aftermath

Life in Munich in the months up to the outbreak of World War I was no less filled by fantasy than his previous existence in Vienna. He had taken lodgings with a tailor named Popp, and he and his wife spoke of him as a voracious reader, broody and eccentric, given to breaking into diatribes against the Jews or Marxism.

Now 25, Hitler was no nearer to a career than at 18, but in August 1914, fate on which he relied with such Micawber-like simplicity, gave him an opportunity with the declaration of war. Hitler threw himself into it with an ardor extraordinary even in those euphoric first days. He promptly addressed a petition to the Kaiser seeking permission, though an Austrian, to join a Bavarian regiment. The disability which had kept him out of the Royal and Imperial Army apparently overlooked, he was drafted into the 1st Company of the 16th Bavarian Infantry Regiment.

As so often happens with personally undisciplined young men, he actually fell into a soldier's life as though he had been waiting for it for years. It may well have been that army life, which as all who have experienced it know, is composed very largely of soul-aching boredom, was for him an opportunity to indulge his penchant for brooding.

Nevertheless, when later he extolled the virtues of military life as that most befitting Germany's young heroes, he cannot be accused of hypocrisy. Whatever else, he did not lack courage. He was twice decorated; the second time with the Iron Cross First Class, having been recommended for it by the regiment's Jewish adjutant. He even refused leave when it was granted. As one of his comrades remarked, his 'regiment was his homeland.'

Serving as a company runner, a notoriously dangerous activity, he got himself such a reputation for having a charmed life that others liked to stay near him. Later he was able to absorb this into his own fantasy-thesis: that fate had singled him out for some special role – the role he had vaguely apprehended from boyhood.

Nonetheless, though his regimental sergeant major, Max Amann, was later to serve the National Socialist cause as its principal publisher and there is an extant photograph of Hitler with two comrades, there is no evidence he formed the close friendships normally associated with army life and shared dangers.

Left: Hitler in 1925 after his release from Landsberg.
Below: Hitler and Streicher (to his right) watch a march past of paraders on German Day in Nuremberg, 1923.
Below right: SA troops march to Munich in 1923 prior to the Putsch.

In 1918 the German Army was thrown by its General Staff into one last grab for victory. At first successful, the daily victories were magnified and gloated over in the press. When the offensive bogged down, under increasing Allied counter-attacks and when these turned into a full blown offensive, there was still no stopping the reports of victories. But the nation was sick of war and as the Americans began arriving in France in increasing numbers, Hindenburg and Ludendorff, the joint commanders of the German forces, if no one else, realized that victory had forever eluded them. When sailors at Kiel mutinied, the commanders' nerves gave out. There was, they advised the government, nothing for it but to request an armistice from the enemy.

Of all this Hitler knew nothing. He was in the hospital at Pasewalk, near Stettin, after having been gassed. Like any other German on the Home Front, his only information was from the newspapers with their accounts of German triumphs. He and his fellow patients listened, hardly believing, as the hospital chaplain brought them the news that the nation had thrown itself on the mercy of its enemies.

Like other Germans, he could think of no other way of explaining this savage and sudden reversal except betrayal made possible by the pacifists, profiteers and Marxists – Jews for the most part – doing their worst at home, while the flower of the nation perished at the front.

All around him, as he convalesced, were the signs that Germany was about to follow Russia into what he saw as the abyss of Bolshevism. The Hitler legend declares that he set his countenance as granite against the Left rabble and, as a result, was arrested, frightening off the detail which had come to fetch him with his rifle. The reality is that it was one of the gangs of extreme Rightists who came for him, after he had registered himself with the army now largely red.

In December 1918 he left the hospital. He volunteered for guard duty at a prisoner of war camp at Traunstein, near the Austrian border, but in January 1919 its last inmates had left. At a loose end, though still in uniform he made his way back to Munich.

It was in the March of that year that Marxism in postwar Europe reached its high tide mark with the '100 Days' of Bela Kun in Hungary. From then on, it slowly receded. Although this resulted as much from the combination of harsh arbitrariness and gross incompetence of the soviets' rule as from any action of the counterrevolutionary forces, it did not prevent those forces from exhibiting the same savage lawlessness they condemned in their adversaries. As the French general Serrigny pointed out in the 1890s: the crisis of discontent always begins behind the lines. This was the case in Russia in 1917: it was similarly the case in Germany. The roots had lain

in the German Navy (another similarity with Russia) bottled up in Kiel by the superior Royal Navy for almost the entire war. It spread among returning prisoners of war from the Russian Front after the Treaty of Brest-Litovsk, and from them to other troops in the rear. The mistake the rebels made was to suppose that those at the front were equally disaffected. This was far from the case. Humane, idealistic and well-intentioned as most of the rebel leadership was, to the veterans of the terrible Western Front battles of 1918, they were merely Home Front shirkers and cowards, who now compounded their felonies with treason, undermining the sacrifices of war. Overly simple and emotional as such an assessment was, it was that made by the majority, including Hitler. The returning soldiers flocked not to the banner of revolution, but to join the various freelancing groups (for example, the *Freikorps*), led by the former officers they had been expected to turn on. They had backing, at first covert, later open, from the rump of *Reichswehr* (the German Army), of which Hitler was still a member.

His uncompromisingly Right Wing views commended themselves to his officers and he was chosen for training in a unit set up to halt the tide of disaffection. His role was small. He spoke occasionally, though always to an official brief, which nonetheless allowed him to express the most violent and insupportable anti-Semitic views. In the presence of his

officers or of social superiors he was obsequious, timid and shuffling, yet it was observed that after meetings there would always be a little group collected around him while he expatiated, lost in the drift of his own words as though drugged, and carrying his little audience with him.

'All over Germany, Munich included, Nationalist groups had sprung up. All had the same objectives, negative rather than positive, those of ridding the country of the 'November traitors' who had brought the disgrace of a dictated peace; of the Marxists, whose loyalties were to an alien power; of the Jews, who had somehow managed to be at the root of all the nation's troubles. Nationalists came from every level of society and the upper middle class. Thule Society represented the highest level.

In Munich at the lower end of the social scale was Anton Drexler's tiny German Workers' Party, to one of whose meetings on 12 September 1919 the 30-year-old Hitler was invited. An indignant outburst during the discussion period so impressed Drexler that he sent him, unasked, a party membership card. As always, Hitler was to claim that he was thrown thereby into an appalling moral dilemma. It seems never to have occurred to him that joining a political party is not quite the same as being awarded, say, a life sentence of imprisonment. If one does not like it, one can leave. In any case, he was not compelled to join simply because he had been sent an unsolicited party card. All that this emphasis on spiritual turmoil illustrates is that the man who so often acted on the inspiration of the moment, when faced with a decision, somehow found his intuition deserted him – a characteristic many were later to discover.

In the end, still a soldier, he joined and, through Drexler's good offices, immediately became a member of its executive committee. A month later, before an audience of 111 people, and now untrammeled by any official brief, he spoke. All his long-suppressed hatreds poured out, especially those naively simplified explanations to which so many had come to attribute their misfortunes – cheating and chicanery by the Jews.

Left: Hitler arrives at Berlin's City Hall to sign the Golden Book.
Right: Hitler speaks to a gathering near Munich in April 1923.

Above: Julius Streicher leads the march in Munich commemorating the 10th anniversary of the Beer Hall Putsch. Hitler and Goering follow closely behind.

This so closely corresponded with the views of his audience that his words were received with enthusiasm. By the end he had made the great discovery of his life: he could speak. The experience was heady enough to one whose spiritual nourishment for a lifetime had been his own fantasies, yet several years were to pass before he began to see himself in the role of absolute political ruler. For a long time he was content to believe himself the John the Baptist of a Messiah yet to reveal himself.

Now at last, he left the army to throw himself into the work of the party, virtually taking it over from the outset. He changed its name to the National Socialist German Workers' Party (Nationalsozialistische Deutsche Arbeiter-Partei or NSDAP); he gave it a program where, hitherto, it had only possessed a set of vague ideals. This was nationalist, anti-Semitic, anticapitalistic, while aiming to gain the support of 'the little man' through such measures as a proposal to communalize the big department stores and rent their departments out to small traders. There were, too, far-reaching land reforms, including the expropriation of land for national purposes, the ending of speculation and the abolition of ground rents.

Most important of all, as propaganda chief, he was able to put into practice cherished theories. He had long held the conviction that the German defeat had largely been the result of British propaganda and had set out to study the methods used. As a result of his conclusion he set out to change the party's image. He designed huge, red posters, with eye-catching slogans and terse, punchy messages; he introduced party uniforms; he had the swastika adopted as symbol. His greatest aim, however, was to replace the small discussion groups with mass meetings. The first, at the *Festsaal* of the Munich *Hofbräuhaus* on 20 February 1920, attracted nearly 2000 people and filled it.

Taking a leaf from the Communists' book, he hired lorries, had them filled with party members who drove noisily through

the streets to meetings. The difference was that while the Communists wore a curious assortment of uniforms or none, the Nazis, many of them old soldiers, sitting bolt upright wore smart uniforms and so seemed the very epitome of law and order reinstated. They were invariably cheered as they passed.

If Hitler could accuse the Left of adopting terror as a political weapon, he was soon surpassing them, seeing, as he later affirmed, that a display of force had its psychological value. It branded the party which used it as a serious organization and not a debating society. It gave the onlooker a feeling of the party's invincibility; it comforted supporters; most of all, a brawl always drew a crowd.

What was more astonishing was that he found the money in Germany's depressed economy for this far from inexpensive pageant. Where it came from has never been settled. At this stage there was certainly less from industry than has been suggested, though some may have come from the secret funds of the *Reichswehr* which, despite its later repudiations, supported Hitler from the moment he looked like presenting a serious challenge to the Left.

Very soon his reputation had spread. Munich society threw open its doors to him; to the Right he was a hero, but even liberals were anxious to meet this young oratorical hypnotist. Hostesses vied for his presence; their female guests competed jealously for his attention.

In appearance he still looked something of an oddity. Now back in civilian clothes, he seemed to have forgotten how to dress. His normal outer garment was a trenchcoat worn with a black velour hat and usually he carried a whip as well. Under this would be a blue suit, sometimes accompanied by a purple shirt, a brown waistcoat and a red tie. Even on social occasions he brought with him his revolver in its holster worn on a leather belt, the entirety being hung on a hatstand before he was ushered into the salon. In company he was awkward and over-deferential, spreading a feeling of uneasiness among his fellow guests like a contagion.

The Right Wing poet, Dietrich Eckart, sought to correct some of these gaucheries and managed to impart to the man he was one of the first to predict would one day be a national leader, a few of the social graces. All the same, he was never relaxed in company and never sought it. When, as head of state he was brought into contact with other heads of state, his relations were always formal. Those about him, whose company he always preferred, were people who he regarded more or less as his social equals.

Below: Goebbels and Himmler watch as Hitler delivers an address to a rally held at Bückeberg in October 1935.

The Leader

Throughout all this Hitler was working with demonic energy. Everything he saw the party was needing he somehow contrived to obtain for it, including a newspaper, the local *Münchener Beobachter*, which under him became the *Völkischer Beobachter* and a national publication with a rapidly rising circulation. And week upon week he fulfilled a killing program of public speaking, ending each meeting physically exhausted by the outpouring of his soul as the applause broke in waves about him.

If there was anything of genius – albeit perverted genius – in Hitler, it was at this time that it became manifest. This was not solely because he turned Anton Drexler's little racist debating club into a political force – though that was achievement enough. Even more it was because of the precision with which he judged the mood of millions of Germans. The NSDAP was never a party in any real sense. Its so-called program was simply bait. It was a lighthouse and what it signaled was a safe haven for every sort of ill-adjusted crank eager to blame his situation on anything except his own deficiencies. No wonder that listening to his speaking, sensitive men, like Albert Speer, felt that Hitler was giving exact verbal form, not to his own original ideas, but to prejudices and hatreds deep within the subconscious of his hearers.

Below: Hitler arrives at the Deutschlandhalle in Berlin to deliver an address in November 1935. Sepp Dietrich and Goebbels grin in the background.

Gradually there began to gather round him those names which would one day be on every lip: Major Ernst Röhm, with his unimpeachable contacts in the *Reichswehr*; Rudolf Hess; Alfred Rosenberg, a Baltic German who had seen something of the Bolshevik Revolution and been left atremble by it; the schoolmaster-pornographer Julius Streicher. Like most men who came after them they encompassed a gamut of half-baked ideas: 'blood and iron' Prussianism; the Teutonic warrior mythos, which, when translated, was to become a new religion; theories of sun worship, vegetarianism and eugenics; and a psychotic hatred of the Jews.

When, in 1921, he came as its most resplendent recruit, Hermann Goering, last commander of Baron von Richthofen's 'flying circus' of fighter aces, was the first to recognize that what passed for the party's ideology was so much 'junk' and being a forthright man, said so. However, by nature a bully, the NSDAP looked like the place for action, and he shared the common hatred of the Jews.

Incredibly, the NSDAP was still more or less of a Bavarian phenomenon (one must remember that then, as now, Germany was a federal state), indeed it had scarcely spread beyond Munich and its environs. It was in correspondence, however, with other Nationalist parties and in 1921 the first tentative moves toward consolidation began. It gave Hitler the opportunity to make himself master of the party. Claiming that he was concerned only with protecting its integrity, he insisted that there must be no question of dilution of its principles by mergers with others; on the contrary, others must come to them. Then it was to be on the basis of individual members who

first resigned from their own parties, and applied to join the NSDAP.

It was a proposition, breath-taking in its audacity to emanate from a minor, largely provincial political organization, and it gave his enemies within the party a chance to try to cut their overweening head of propaganda down to size. All the signs are that Hitler was waiting for just such a showdown, yet it was at this moment he took himself off to Berlin. Here he was horrified by what he found as he had been earlier in Vienna. The capital was to him corruption personified, not just a new Babylon, but Sodom and Gomorrah to boot and he railed against it with evangelistic zeal at a series of successful meetings, never failing to point to the Jews as the maggots in the core.

In the meantime, in Munich, just what he must have anticipated was happening. Under pressure, Drexler was beginning negotiations with other Nationalist parties of just the sort Hitler had set his face against. When he heard of this, Hitler himself, who had arranged to be kept informed, returned to Munich and threw down his resignation. As he hoped, consternation reigned. The party simply could not sacrifice the man who had made it. He took advantage of this to offer his colleagues the chance to redeem themselves – by giving him dictatorial power. In the mood of general repentance, he got all he asked for. He had used for the first time the tactic he was to exploit so successfully: that of first provoking and then mastering a crisis. All that remained was the problem of Drexler. As founder of the party he could scarcely be expelled or even superseded. The answer was found in the device of making him president and hence a powerless, constitutional head of the party.

At a meeting on 29 July in which the party committee was changed so as to pack it with his own supporters, Hitler was rapturously greeted for the first time as *Unser Führer* – Our Leader. A month later, he bolstered up his power in a totally different way. The SA (*Sturm Abteilung* translates as Storm Detachments or Storm Troopers) was created. Ostensibly the excuse was that while the Right Wing para-military groups had been hounded and finally quashed by the government, those of the Left had been permitted to survive and were continuing their harassment and terror. To this accusation there was at this time less substance than hitherto, though there was some.

Anyway, the ostensible reason bore no relation to the real one. The SA was to be, in part, a private army to be schooled for the seizure of power, if force were necessary; in part, a show of the kind of uniformed and therefore official-looking brutality Hitler believed would impress friends and foes alike. Very soon they were to be seen, not just in the streets of Munich, but all over Bavaria, marching columns of men, bawling out the party songs with their violent threats, handing out party leaflets, ripping down the posters of rivals. When, as quickly happened, they got a reputation for brawling and for threatening enemies, Hitler, far from denying, proudly acknowledged it. Not even collecting boxes which invited the public to subscribe to 'The Massacre of the Jews' were with-

Below: The Führer watches a Hitler Youth parade on Labor Day 1935 with Goebbels, von Schirach and Hess behind.

drawn. At party meetings they adopted, under Hitler's tutelage, a strategy of defense by attack. A heckler had barely to open his mouth before being surrounded by a throng of the peak-capped, brown-tunicked SA men with flailing fists.

There were, undoubtedly, times when such tactics were necessary if Nazi speakers were to get a hearing. There were many others when such shows of naked aggression were used as propagandistic terror.

In 1922, one such display resulted in Hitler's paying his first visit to prison. The Nazis had broken up a meeting of one of its political adversaries and assaulted its leader. Perhaps because for the first time the authorities had evidence on which to prosecute and anyway wanted to show they still had teeth, Hitler found himself in court. He was sentenced to three months' imprisonment, but served only four weeks and was released to a rapturous welcome.

Once free he recommenced his program of public speaking now virtually non-stop, sometimes addressing six, even seven meetings in a single night. The party, too, was coming to be nationally recognized, if scarcely, among its more sedate and better-established rivals, taken as a serious threat.

With another of history's 'ifs' we can have very little doubt about the answer. By the early 1920s, despite all that had happened, there were signs of returning stability in Germany, including economic stability. If this had persisted there is no doubt that National Socialism would have atrophied as a pass-

ing phenomenon, unpleasant enough but far from dangerous in any real sense. What gave it continued life was the great inflation whose tornadolike upward spiral began in 1921.

At the onset of this economic crisis there came a blow to the already tender national pride. When there was a defaulting in reparations' payments, France occupied the Ruhr, the great industrial basin and claimed for itself goods and plant to the value of what was owed. The government, powerless with the purely token forces it was allowed under the peace treaty, protested, then ordered its employees in the Ruhr to carry out a policy of non-cooperation and passive resistance. The French responded with draconian measures including military tribunals which handed down ten and 20 year sentences. Germans, old enough to have experienced both, still speak of this period as infinitely worse than the Red Army's occupation immediately after World War II.

Many leading Nazis were later to claim to have played a leading part in a heroic resistance movement. (One was Goebbels who said he had acquired his clubfoot as a result of injuries. The story was totally without foundation.) Ironically enough, Hitler actually ordered that members of the party should play no part in resistance, as by doing so they would have to unite with other political forces and thereby risk loss of identity. In fact, he saw the French Occupation as one more pressure on the hated republic, perhaps bringing it down, and so throwing Germany's entire political future into the melting

pot. He would not take any action that could delay this end.

What, in any event, the French act amounted to was a renewal of hostilities. Whatever else happened in the nation's life, it happened against the awareness that part of its territory was under 'enemy' occupation. At the same time, with the seizure of so much of its industrial output and the heart of German industry, the ailing mark began its uncontrollable plummet. A lifetime's saving became valueless in days. Stamps were overprinted with sums which a few years earlier would have bought a mansion; then overprinted again with still higher sums. The German middle class, cautious, thrifty and motivated by an almost blind sense of duty became totally dispossessed and consequently embittered. The only industry not depressed was printing. It simply could not keep up with the flow of notes required.

Yet for some inflation brought great advantages: speculating against their own currency some Germans made fortunes; in other cases, borrowings made when the mark was at a higher value could quite easily be repaid when it dropped. More seriously, it seemed to many that inflation was simply the device of the government to offload its reparation debts. As the mark fell against world currencies the sum which had to be repaid to the victorious allies was also reduced. Since the ordinary Germans believed these dishonorable debts were the result of government pusillanimity, they felt that the government's obligations were being fulfilled at their expense.

Above: Hitler inspects the autobahn in 1938.

When Hitler swore, as he ceaselessly did, that once in power the party would tear up the Treaty of Versailles which contained these disgraceful clauses, he was cheered to the echo. Party membership numbers shot up like a pious soul making for heaven. And it was at this time that Hitler saw himself as the future ruler of Germany – Führer not just to the NSDAP, but to the nation.

The spur was Mussolini, who in 1922 had staged his successful march on Rome. The German Nationalist movement was fired with envious admiration, those of Bavaria seeing what had happened in Italy, the takeover of the capital and its government by provincial patriots, as a particularly apt example to them.

Hitler, for his part, was in a dither of frustration. On the one hand was Mussolini's achievement; on the other his own impotence, while the Bavarian government was beginning to lean heavily on the National Socialists, banning meetings, demonstrations and speakers and making a mustering of its forces impossible. On top of this was his ever-present fear that the national government might take some action which would bring the entire people behind it in support. Realizing that nothing could be done without assistance, he threw the party into a union which was being formed of all the Nationalist groups – the so-called *Kampfbund* (League for Struggle).

From the spring on, he employed every resource and every ounce of influence he possessed to try to bring it round to the idea of a 'March on Berlin.' His contacts included the *Reichswehr*'s General Officer Commanding in Bavaria, General von Lossow who, at one stage, he was visiting almost daily. Late that month, with a story about a planned Left coup to be launched on May Day, he demanded access to the arms stored in the barracks so that the Nazis could break up the traditional Labor Day parades which were to serve as the spark. Lossow refused. His forces, he declared, were quite capable of dealing with any outbreak of trouble.

Not to be balked, the party began gathering its own not inconsiderable secret arms stocks. (Among these was a machine gun brought to Munich by a pedantic young man named Heinrich Himmler.) These were augmented when Röhm, the head of the SA, bluffed his way into the armory and helped himself.

As the trade unions and other delegations began their demonstrations – perfectly peacefully and with not the slightest sign that this was the beginning of a coup, the Nazis themselves assembled on a parade ground outside the city. That was as far as they got. Röhm, who was to have given the signal to start the attack, failed to arrive. The theft from the armory discovered, he was actually in front of an enraged Lossow. When he arrived at about noon, it was in the company of detachments of the army which cordoned off the entire area. Hitler was forced to surrender and only the internal crisis within the country and the government's unwillingness to provoke any action against itself prevented reprisals.

To Landsberg Prison

Hitler was totally downcast by the turn events had taken and for a time believed all his hopes were dashed. When he was threatened with prosecution, however, he summoned up enough spirit to answer it with a letter which made it clear that his trial would be turned into a patriotic demonstration.

In any case, despite his impatience, time was actually on his side. What little unity the French action in the Ruhr had inspired was quickly evaporating as the occupation dragged on and the government showed itself impotent.

By August of 1922, he was back in the saddle, and in September, the government gave him an opening: it called off the campaign of passive resistance. Notwithstanding his earlier disdain he now exploited the opportunity to accuse the government of cowardice. In this he had support in high places. Conflict between the Social Democrat Government of Bavaria and the District Command of the *Reichswehr* had reached the point at which the federal authorities had decided to suspend the *Land* government. In its place a State Commissioner was appointed in the person of Gustav Kahr. Since he was himself a Right Wing Nationalist his appointment had actually brought about another conflict – between himself and Social Democrat Berlin. This the National Socialists, through their newspaper, *Völkischer Beobachter*, did their best to foment and succeeded when demands from Berlin for the newspaper's suppression were ignored.

In his refusal to be dictated to from the capital Kahr had gathered round him two powerful supporters, Lossow and the head of the State police, Seisser. How near the situation was coming to open civil war is indicated by the fact that Kahr actually ordered the increasing of the border guard between Bavaria and its neighboring provinces.

Moderate elements talked of a separation of the province from Germany, the less moderate revived the notion of the 'March on Berlin.' It was this alone which interested Hitler, but it was soon plain that the State Commissioner and his associates had ruled it out. He, therefore, began making his own plans. The *Kampfbund* was to rally its entire forces, seize Munich's keypoints and force the trio to take sides in what appeared to be a revolutionary *fait accompli*. The original date set for this was 10 November, but it was moved back two days

when it was announced that all three would be at a big meeting at the Munich *Bürgerbräu Keller*. Hitler believed its purpose was to announce the first step toward a declaration of Bavarian independence.

He summoned his own forces, burst in brandishing a revolver and, while some of his supporters took over the meeting, compelled Kahr, Seisser and Lossow into another room at gun point. There he tried unsuccessfully to persuade them to join the revolt he assured them was already in train. When they were unmoved he went back to the hall and calmly announced that the Bavarian government had been removed and that he proposed a new one whose first duty was to march 'on that sinful Babylon, Berlin' and there establish a national government.

It was the cheering which greeted this that first caused the men in the side room to waver. At this moment one of the men who was to form Hitler's 'new government,' General Erich Ludendorff arrived and at once urged them to adopt a policy of compliance. All then agreed to participate in Hitler's plan. Everybody returned to the hall where hands were publicly shaken and in a brief but rousing address Hitler described the moment as a vindication of that time when he had lain 'a blind cripple' in the military hospital at Pasewalk while the 'November criminals' gave away his own and Germany's birthright.

After unavoidable delays, the crowd in the *bierkeller* formed up outside to be joined by some 600 Stormtroopers, and with eyes turned in the direction of Berlin the march began. They had not gone far when they were stopped by the police. Here, while Goering threatened, the rest pushed them aside and continued on their way. But at the *Odeonplatz*, one of Munich's main squares, there was another police cordon. Among the

Below: General von Reichenau and Hitler watch troop maneuvers in Poland in September 1939 as Himmler and General von Manstein watch enthusiastically (left).
Overleaf: Hitler passes packed throngs in Berlin in the Victory Parade in 1940 celebrating Germany's triumph in the West.

overwrought crowd a single shot rang out, perhaps intended as a warning. It was followed, however, by an exchange at the end of which 14 members of the crowd and three policemen lay dead or seriously wounded, and the procession was effectively broken up.

Hitler, in the meantime, had vanished – a fact he was to find difficult to explain away later. Only one person was left – Ludendorff – who had apparently decided to continue the march on his own. Not until second thoughts had prevailed or he had realized that even he could hardly form a government unaided did he give himself up to the nearest policeman.

What followed was, of course, Hitler's second visit to jail, but he managed to turn the trial into a Nazi rally so successful, the prosecutor found himself virtually apologizing. He was given a five year sentence with eligibility for parole after six months. When he reached prison he was treated like royalty in exile. He was excused from labor, dined surrounded by his cronies under a swastika banner, was allowed parcels and visits without restriction and, as the world now knows, was perfectly free to embark upon the writing of that egregious document *Mein Kampf*.

In late 1924 he was released. During his sojourn in prison, however, events had turned against him and his movement – a factor which had led to an early release, since he was no longer considered a menace. The French were beginning to evacuate the Ruhr, the inflation had been pegged, the Dawes Plan offered a way out of the impasse of reparations payments, the number of unemployed was dropping. In his absence, the National Socialists and most of the other groups making up the *Kampfbund* had splintered and its members scattered. As he left prison this time there were no cheering crowds, just a car and a handful of well-wishers. All this was reflected in the 1924 elections in which the Nationalist parties were routed.

Under the new *Land* government in Bavaria, the National Socialist Party and its organ, *Völkischer Beobachter*, had been proscribed. Hitler, determined to build anew needed the free-

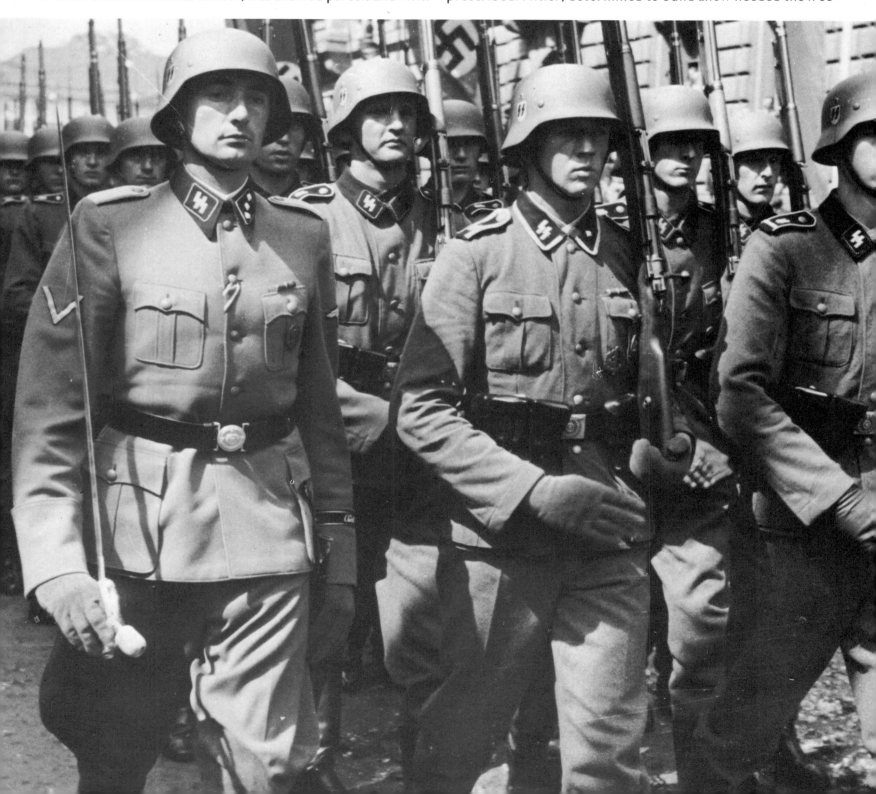

dom to organize his party and to publish its newspaper. At the same time he needed to bring together the rump of the *Kampfbund* as the nucleus of a new movement.

His attempts to prove to the government that he was a true blue legalist for whom the debacle of November 1923 had been an aberration never to be repeated was sufficiently successful for them to remove the ban on the party in early 1925. On 25 February, the *Beobachter* appeared on the streets announcing a meeting at the *Bürgerbräu Keller*, starting point of the earlier disaster. At a gathering which included representatives of the groups making up the *Kampfbund* he employed his usual tactic of provoking a crisis: either they must accept him as overall leader of an admittedly virtually leaderless national coalition or it ceased to exist.

He did this after a speech in which he emphasized the terrible menaces facing the nation, most fearful of which was that posed by Jewish machinations, through Marxism, unrestricted capitalism and, especially, bastardization of the Aryan race.

At its end the audience, jumping on tables to clap and cheer, were practically begging him to accept the responsibilities of leadership. After the meeting letters of support poured in from all over Germany. In the weeks that followed Hitler gave every sign that his conversion to democratic legalism had been a complete one. Instead of scorning parliament and its electoral rites, the National Socialists prepared to support and actively participate in them.

While waiting for this first test of strength among the voters, Hitler gave his mind to another problem. He had long been exercised by the SA and its leader, Röhm, whose eyes were set so unswervingly on the regular army that he saw the SA merely as adjunct to it. There had even been talk of it as a 'secret reserve' for the regular forces. If, in a crisis the SA should come under army orders, it would obviously be lost to Hitler. What he saw was needed, therefore, was a body inextricably linked to his own person. Out of this sprang the SS (*Schutz Staffeln* translates as Protection Squads), which at first numbered only 200 men drawn from the *Stoss Truppe Hitler* of the SA and led by Erhard Heiden. It was not until 1929 that Heiden was replaced by Himmler who turned it into the Order of Dominicans of the Third Reich.

From its inception, Munich had been the home of the party and now as it became a nationwide movement, this had remained the case. There were, however, mutterings of discontent arising mainly from the severe distrust felt toward many of Hitler's headquarters' associates by other party branches. In Thuringia, which borders on Bavaria, this was turning into a serious challenge not just to Munich's hegemony, but to the policies emanating from there.

The head of the party in the province was Gregor Strasser, whose closest associates were his brother, Otto, and a young novelist-manqué with a limp, Paul Josef Goebbels. All three were unswervingly loyal to Hitler, but believed the party to lack a program and insofar as it had affirmed any principles these had tended away from rather than toward the kind of Left, though admittedly nationalistic, revolution the three believed in.

This omission they themselves set out to rectify, convinced that Hitler would be won over once he could be separated from his Munich clique. Basically, they believed that Germany's orientation must be toward the Soviet Revolution, but in detail their aims were little more than a reshuffling of ideas from various sections of radical Left.

That their activities at first passed unnoticed was because Hitler was at that time involved in strictly personal affairs. He had just rented a country house at Berchtesgaden in the Bavarian Alps and given the running of it to his half-sister, Angela. This brought him into constant contact with her pretty daughter, Angelika or 'Geli.' He quickly became infatuated, while she, at first uninterested, even perhaps repelled by the older man's advances, gradually began to soften toward him. The whole affair was marked, however, by his hesitancy which he, on his side, attributed to the fact that he was, technically at least, her uncle. Although, as the Soviet pathologist's post mortem report shows, Hitler did not have the underdeveloped genitalia popularly ascribed to him, there are signs, if not of psychological impotence, at any rate of problems in that area. This would be wholly consistent with his parent relationship. If, in the conflicts between mother and father he had been protected by his coddling mother, prolongation of the Œdipus stage would have made it difficult for him to form normal sexual relationships. And this, of itself, is consistent with his prudery, his readiness to imagine sexual

Left: Troops of the SS Leibstandarte Adolf Hitler parade in Berlin during the victory celebrations of 1940.

seduction of gentile girls as the underlying strategy of Jewish world-conspiracies and his exaggerated conduct toward women.

Whatever his relationship with Geli Raubal may have been, however, he had to tear himself away from her when the Thuringian group declared that, in the advancement of their political aims, all means were permissible, including, where necessary, terrorism. This, of course, ran quite counter to his new-found stance of legalism, but there was something which touched him more directly: he was, after all, still on parole from a five year sentence. If the authorities thought his followers were still liable to practice violent methods, he might well find himself clapped back in jail.

A meeting of all party leaders was summoned at Bamberg. Its excuse was that a matter of policy touching the estates of Germany's former princes had to be thrashed out. These had been confiscated with the formation of the republic in 1918 and the question now was: were they to be given back or finally expropriated? To the horror of the Thuringian group, and especially the young Goebbels, Hitler was for restitution. The fact was that he hoped for some advantage from grateful royalty, but his excuse was that it was the grossest of hypocrisies to confiscate the property of good Germans when that of Jewish bankers was left untouched. That was not all. He also made perfectly clear that it was he alone who made party policy and that he was quite happy with it as it was.

The message that the party was intended to be no more than the janissaries of the inspired will of its leader had not yet struck home. His success at Bamberg was no less complete than it had been on other occasions, yet he showed an uncharacteristic inclination to be conciliatory. When Gregor Strasser was injured in an accident, he rushed to the hospital to visit him bearing a big bouquet of flowers. Later, he appointed him head of party propaganda.

The fact was that he had spotted a rare talent among the rebels in its most vituperatively radical member, Josef Goebbels. Soon after, by cajolery, charm and flattery, he won him over so successfully that he completely abandoned his Left-radical stance. In the fall of 1926 Goebbels got his reward. The Berlin party, and especially its SA, had long been a thorn in the flesh of headquarters and, at that time, was openly mutinous. Hitler made Goebbels *gauleiter* of the capital with powers which were greater than those of any of his counterparts and sent him off to clean up. The success Goebbels' ruthless methods achieved marked him down for later favor, particularly since he combined them with an abject adoration of his Führer.

However, to ensure that there was no repetition of the Strasser revolt with local *gauleiters* getting above themselves, a party called USCHLA (*Untersuchungs- und Schlichtungs-Ausschuss* translates as Committee for Investigation and Settlement) was established.

Munich to Berlin

In the nation at large circumstances were no longer so favorable to the party. For all the activity, for all the campaigns and the recruiting drives which now took the party officials among those they had previously ignored, membership was declining and interest waning. In this atmosphere, the governments of Bavaria and Saxony which had placed a restriction on Hitler's addressing public meetings, rescinded it.

A meeting at Munich's *Krone Kirkus* held in the spring of 1927 filled the auditorium and contained many of the old elements of pageantry with phalanxes of uniformed SA men marching down the main aisle led by drummers while Hitler returned the Roman salute they had just begun to copy from the Italian *fascisti*. His address was cheered to the echo, but in long term results it produced nothing.

Very soon, indeed, Hitler, making a virtue of necessity, began to speak of the NSDAP as a small, elite force of around 100,000 members. That way, he declared, it would remain manageable.

To emphasize the decline in their fortunes, in the Reichstag elections of May 1928 they received only 2.6 percent of the vote, although a group of National Socialist deputies, among them Goebbels, took their place in the House for the first time.

At this juncture, the National Socialists, who thrived on such things, were given a fresh lease on life by a new national crisis. The Dawes Plan, which had simply provided a schedule of payments for reparations, was succeeded by the Young Plan. Although this gave a wider measure of freedom to Germany than had existed under the Dawes Plan, its computations still envisaged Germans paying out for a period which was estimated at 60 years. Thus, the grandchildren of those yet unborn would be inheritors of debts they had no part in contracting. Though the sums were small and there was never any evidence that reparations affected the German economy in the slightest, they still gave a heaven-sent opportunity to the Nationalists.

Using this as his lever, Hitler now set out to propel his still largely provincial party into the national arena. The opportunity presented itself when he attached it to a temporary coalition of the Right formed to contest the plan. Among the leaders of this was Alfred Hugenberg, a former Krupps' director, now master of his own industrial empire which included several successful newspapers and the UFA film company, subsequently to be the tool of Goebbels's propaganda apparat.

The alliance not only brought Hitler into contact with respectable and influential figures – Hugenberg was among other things a Privy Councillor. It also provided the party with funds. These had to be used, of course, for the campaign against the Young Plan. Hitler was, nonetheless, cock-a-hoop as the symbols of the NSDAP began to appear in large numbers all over Germany. Goebbels was appointed head of propaganda, in succession to Strasser, and set to work with the same energy with which he had cleared out the Augean stables of the Berlin party. It was soon clear that in every respect, the propaganda efforts of the Nazis totally outstripped the insipid offerings of their allies. At the same time, they made very little secret of their contempt for these 'moth-eaten eagles' as Goebbels called them.

The fact that the campaign failed in its purpose was to Hitler of small importance. It was even an advantage in that it left the grievance festering. Publicized through the Hugenberg press, he was now a national figure for the first time.

This, in its turn, had the effect of bringing him new connections, especially among the important business and financial community. The coffers of the party which had rattled so emptily a few months before were soon overflowing. All he wanted achieved, and on the excuse that now the campaign was over the *raison d'etre* for an alliance with the bourgeois parties no longer existed, Hitler severed his link with Hugenberg. During the period of their association, the NSDAP had probably made more impact as a serious political force than at any time in its entire previous existence. With the transfusion of fresh funds into its kitty, the party began fighting elections on a scale never before envisaged. In Thuringia it even managed to obtain its first ministry in the *Land* government.

If there were those among its opponents who hoped that this was all a mere flash in the pan, or pointed to the fact that by the standards of the longer-established, traditional parties

Below: Hitler gives an address to massed thousands in Berlin and millions listening in by radio soon after the outbreak of war in 1939.

the Nazis were still insignificant, they were soon to be undeceived. In 1929 came the New York Stock Exchange collapse and the Depression. Economic self-confidence in Germany was too friable and too short-lived not to be hit. The numbers of men on the dole increased. By September 1930 they had reached three million, only to double in the next two years, and it was estimated at that time that half the families in the country were affected.

Set beside this, all previous crises were as nothing. And Hitler made the fullest possible use of it. Flogging himself tirelessly in a round of meetings and addresses, always with unfailing insight touching the raw and fearful nerves of every sector of German society, he brought more and more under the party's banner. There they were encouraged to find the antidote to whatever was their own particular anxiety.

In factories and offices, in competition with the Communist cells, the Nazis began organizing their own; agitators stopped to talk to men waiting outside the Labor Exchanges, gaining their confidence, then giving them literature specially produced for the purpose. The party had taken off. It was drawing in members from every walk of society and every age group.

There were, of course, those who sought to combat it. The Communists took the lead in trying to warn people of the true character of National Socialism by reference to past statements and actions of its leaders, particularly Hitler and Goering. In some areas there was a recrudescence of street fighting as in the immediate postwar years. The Nazis, if anything, turned this to their own advantage.

Most of all the party was appealing to the young, especially through the universities where students flocked to join, in some cases threatening the lives of academics who did not emulate them or who refused to denounce their Jewish colleagues. The party encouraged this picture of itself as the movement of youth and the future by pointing out in its propaganda how many young men held high office within the party in comparison with the aged leadership to be found in their rivals.

In the run up campaign to the Reichstag election of September 1930, the National Socialists, led by Hitler, worked as never before. Every trick was employed, from cities down to the smallest hamlets the party's great red posters were to be seen, often with Hitler staring from them, mouth set grimly and eyes looking sternly forward. The biggest halls were booked everywhere and filled. There were open air meetings not only by day but also by night with torches carried by SA men to illuminate the scene. Cavalcades of poster bedecked cars drove through the remotest areas. In all Goebbels, who masterminded the entire campaign, organized some 6000 mass meetings and, with Hitler, spoke at so many that by polling day, hoarse and exhausted, they could only sit back and await the results.

These outstripped all hopes. In the Reichstag, the NSDAP with 107 seats, was second only to the Social Democrats with 143. The Communists came in a poor third with 77. Most of the men whose names had become synonymous with National Socialism were now party deputies in the nation's parliament. (Hitler never stood. This was not simply because his eyes were set on higher things; it was mainly because as an Austrian he was not eligible.)

While the National Socialists were celebrating their gains, Heinrich Brüning, the Social Democrat Chancellor, was faced with an appalling predicament. Not only did he not command an absolute majority, but there was obviously no way, in view of the political mix, that he could hope to get one.

The way out he chose was one which gave Hitler his prece-

Left: A youthful supporter presents a bouquet to Hitler.

dent later. He and his Cabinet acted more or less as 'advisers' to the President, Field Marshal von Hindenburg, who maintained continuity of government through 'presidential decrees.' The ensuing policies were, indeed, little more than austerity and belt-tightening did not inspire confidence and Brüning was the butt of his political enemies, in particular, the Nazis.

Nowhere was the disparity of age more marked than between the National Socialist leaders and the incumbent of the Presidency. Field Marshal Paul von Beneckendorf und Hindenburg was 82 and his election in 1925 had been due partially to his role as joint Commander in Chief of the German forces from 1916. (Nominally, he was Conmander in Chief, Ludendorff was his Quartermaster General, but all decisions were taken by the latter, though their combined signature HL was appended to actual orders.) He was a gruff, not unkindly old soldier with an unfeigned love for his people, which was accompanied by a hearty loathing of Hitler – 'the Bohemian corporal' as he called him – a feeling to be confirmed by coming events.

In 1932, the *Ersatz Kaiser*, as Hindenburg was universally dubbed, was up for reelection. Brüning, unwilling to expose the nation to turmoils of an election at such a time, wanted to amend the Constitution so as to extend the period of presidential office. But to do this he required the cooperation of the National Socialist deputies in the Reichstag. They, for their part, could only refuse to take so momentous a decision. He was compelled, therefore, to go to Hitler who since early 1931 had been living in the Hotel Kaiserhof in Berlin, believing the summons to power not far off.

For him the dilemma was that if he refused Brüning's proposal it would look like a personal affront to the one trusted and revered figure in German politics. If, on the other hand, he accepted it he would be sacrificing the opportunity to stand for the presidency himself at the time when, thanks to Brüning's introduction of rule-by-decree it was the seat of absolute power.

In the end, and after the usual harrowing soul-searching, the chance of gaining power proved too much and he refused his party's support. The implied insult to the old man was cleverly riposted by a campaign to 'expose' the proposed constitutional change as a device by Brüning to stay in office at all costs and hence prolong the misery of the German people.

Next came the dilemma of whether Hitler himself should actually stand, which again would seem like an affront to Hindenburg. Up to three weeks before polling day he remained undecided. The truth was that it was less the fear of upsetting the president than of suffering a humiliating defeat which made him hesitate. Once he was satisfied there was little danger of this he went ahead.

What followed was a presidential campaign such as the country had never before experienced. The red party posters were now becoming a familiar sight and added to these, every contrivance of modern publicity was employed, sometimes for the first time. Newspapers were bombarded with stories and photographs, fifty thousand records of a speech were distributed to almost every leading person in the country. There was even a ten minute film shown at specially set up open air cinemas.

But the most ingenious innovation of all was the use of aircraft to convey Hitler from meeting to meeting, which often took place on opposites sides of the country. Never had such a thing been attempted. He was seen by and addressed more people than any politician had before in any country in the world. It also gave Goebbels the opening for his slogan 'Hitler Over Germany' with its ingenious double meaning. The night before the election Goebbels' paper *Der Angriff* was predicting: 'Tomorrow Hitler Will Be President!'

Young supporters greet Der Führer as he arrives for an SS meeting in Berlin. Himmler lurks behind.

It was premature. The result, on 13 March, while not the feared humiliating defeat – Hitler got just over 30 percent of the vote and was in second place – gave Hindenburg a 49.6 percent lead. Yet he had not got the necessary absolute majority and so the whole process had to be repeated on 10 April. Hitler's share of the vote rose to 36.8 percent, but Hindenburg, with 53 percent, now had the clear lead he needed. (The only remaining candidate, the Communist Ernst Thälmann registered only 10.2 percent.)

The Portals of Power

Looked at in retrospect, the achievement seems amazing. The mind harks back to the timorous Hitler of the Vienna and early Munich days, the broody corporal, the struggling Munich politician. In fact, at the time, when set beside their grandiose expectations, it was a bitter disappointment to the National Socialists and a cause for rejoicing among their rivals. The situation was made worse for Hitler by the suicide of Geli Raubal at this time, a tragedy from which he never fully recovered.

Brüning felt confident enough to take measures against the Nazis and ordered the disbandment of the SA and SS, under a decree which prohibited uniformed political organizations. This was followed by police swoops to ensure the ban was

respected. In some SA quarters there was an inclination to stand and fight, but Hitler immediately overruled this.

People other than the Nazis were involved, however. Many of the Rightist and Nationalist bodies had their own uniforms, including some, like the *Stahlhelm* (Steel Helmet) which were ostensibly veterans' organizations and could, therefore, represent what had happened as an insult to those who had fought for Germany. This, they perfectly well knew, would have its appeal to the president.

The repercussions of Brüning's seemingly straight-forward act resounded throughout Germany, with Groener, his Defense Minister and architect of the ban, on the receiving end of much abuse. Between Hindenburg and his Chancellor the issue was a further irritant in an increasingly antagonistic relationship and on 30 May, in a gesture reminiscent of the late Russian tsar, the *Ersatz Kaiser* dismissed him, and the government resigned. One of the charges against Brüning was that his government had included 'Bolsheviks' by which no doubt Groener was meant. What followed was a government far more to the President's taste led by Franz von Papen and, since it contained a heavy sprinkling of landowners, like Hindenburg himself, called the 'Cabinet of Barons.'

On 16 June, the ban on SS and SA uniforms was lifted, though not before the Nazis had provoked the government to action by publicly wearing them. The fact that he had to be thus compelled to repeal the decree, did not stop Papen from asking Hitler for a *quid pro quo*. This was nothing less than his support for a future government led by Papen. Hitler told him there would be time enough to decide this after the elections, which were to take place in July.

Hitler arrives at the Bückeburg rally in October 1935. Krause, his aide, stands to the right.

With the Nazis back in uniform and with the dazzling prospect of power before them, could they but maintain the state of disorder which made government impossible, there was now virtual civil war in parts of Germany. The army had frequently to intervene in clashes between Nazis and Communists and in one incident when 7000 Nazis marched provocatively through a largely Communist working class area there was shooting on both sides. Some 17 people were killed, besides other casualties, some serious.

At a time when a succession of German politicians had found the weight of their existing responsibilities more than enough, Papen actually decided to increase his. In what he thought would be an authoritarian gesture sufficient to impress the Nazis and win their support he dismissed the *Land* government of Prussia in which Berlin stood and assumed control himself. The significance of this was that it gave him mastery of the state police, a power not to be relinquished by his successors.

The elections took place on 31 July. When the results were announced they showed that the Nazis had overtaken the entire field. With 13,745,000 votes they had 230 seats in the Reichstag. The National Socialists were the biggest single party in the 608 member House. Yet Hitler took his time before responding to this change in party fortunes and it was not until 5 August that, as leader of the biggest group, he went to demand the Chancellorship for himself and the key portfolios for his nominees. Hindenburg demurred. If Hitler wanted to be Chancellor it must be over a coalition which commanded the overall support of the Reichstag. Negotiations were protracted, but at their end a furious Hitler, refusing all but total power, stormed out.

With no possiblity of forming a workable coalition, there was no alternative but a further period of government by presidential decree, with Papen, of whom Hindenburg was particularly fond, continuing as Chancellor. But his situation was not quite the same as Brüning's: the National Socialists and the Communists acting together could block any measure he wished to take. As each hoped to benefit from the collapse of the government, this incongruous alliance became, not merely possible, but actual.

On 12 September the new Reichstag assembled for the first time. The Communist, Torgler, almost as a matter of form, moved a vote of censure on the government as an amendment to the Order of the Day. Few among the old political hands even took it seriously. Then, Goering, who had been elected President, announced that a vote was to be taken. Papen rose to demand the floor, but in vain. Goering made out not to see him. Even when Papen took the decree of dissolution from his portfolio and waved it under the President's nose he was still ostentatiously ignored. When the voting was completed it was found that the Communist motion had been carried by 512 votes to 32. Papen had been dismissed and the newly elected Reichstag had existed for something less than an hour.

If the National Socialists hoped to gain further at the polls, they were disappointed. Though they remained the largest party in the assembly, their portion of seats dropped from over 37 percent to about 33.5 percent. They now had 196 deputies out of a total of 584. But they had also lost two million

Hitler delivers his
speech to the Party

votes, while other parties, including the Communists with 100 seats, had made gains.

Papen made a further effort to form a government by wooing Hitler, but when his suit was rejected, admitted defeat and Hindenburg appointed the intriguer, General Kurt von Schleicher, his Chancellor.

As each fresh performer in this parliamentary vaudeville took the stage, the National Socialists could hope that their own turn was coming nearer. But the question of the moment for them was whether they could survive until it did. They were desperately short of funds and had the debts incurred in successive elections. To loosen the purse strings of wealthy, potential supporters they needed to show they were real contenders for power. What was more they had actually alienated many of the people who could help them by their strident condemnation of the Papen government as a reactionary clique. This sounded ominously like the language of the Left to many ears and to strengthen this suspicion they had come out in support of an especially violent Berlin transport strike – not because they wanted to, but because they had to. Failure would have risked the loss of working class support.

Within the party itself, too, there was seething discontent and the growing belief that Hitler was frittering away the chance of power. For weeks the SA had been standing to around Berlin in case its armed assistance was needed, but protracted inactivity was breeding a mood of rebelliousness.

Schleicher, meanwhile, was trying to form his own power base by uniting the elements in the nation. But they were by now too far apart to be brought together by one man: the business world, suspicious of labor, wanted a government which would leave them unfettered – as they believed – to rebuild the economy; the Trade Unions, suspicious of big business, refused to compromise their own freedom of maneuver.

In a bid to court the National Socialists, Schleicher went not to Hitler, who had already proved so intransigent, but to Gregor Strasser. For a few days there was confusion. At one point Hitler may even have gone so far as to have given him permission to join the Schleicher Cabinet as a means of gaining a toe hold on power.

Whatever the truth of this may have been, there was certainly a total reversal at a meeting held at the Hotel Kaiserhof in December 1932. Strasser found himself assailed from all sides and was accused of rank disloyalty to the Führer. Finally, he quietly slipped out and disappeared to Italy on holiday with his family. If he ever felt the temptation to exploit the opportunity Schleicher had given him, thus splitting the party down the middle and perhaps emerging as leader, he controlled it. He was too loyal a man for such subterfuges.

Hitler felt no such constraints of loyalty. He assiduously set about smashing Strasser's power within the party. In 1934 he had him executed.

The incident had, of course, done nothing to heal either the fundamental breaches inside the party or to improve its financial situation. A dramatic change in the latter took place after a meeting between Hitler and the Cologne banker, Kurt von Schroeder. As a result of it Hitler was put in touch with a number of leading bankers and businessmen who came forward to help the party. The principal purpose of it had, however, been to bring Hitler and Papen together in an effort to resolve some of the differences separating them in order that they might unite in a government.

When he heard of it, Schleicher was beside himself with fury and went immediately to Hindenburg to complain, although when Papen appeared before the president he was adamant that their meeting was not aimed against the present Chancellor.

Schleicher had other troubles. His attempt to win over the population at large to his measures had caused him to run foul of a powerful minority – the Junker landowners. For years

Below: Hitler speaks to Albert Bormann, Martin's brother, on the Day of German Art in Munich.

120

they had been receiving special subsidies from the government, the so-called *Osthilfe*, originally meant to stop the threatened destruction of German agriculture at the height of the economic crisis. It had long since become the means of enrichment for landowners at the expense of the hated republic. Schleicher had threatened an investigation and in so doing incurred the wrath of the President, himself a landowner. Faced by implacable hostility for his measures from the employers and now the landowners, Schleicher next addressed himself to the Social Democrats. They could no more bring themselves to trust him than anyone else.

Hitler, for his part, was still looking for the unequivocal triumph, even if a minor one, which would put his credentials for leadership beyond dispute among his own followers and impress on outsiders that he was still a force to be reckoned with. It came with the provincial government election in the small *Land* of Lippe. In a campaign without precedence in scale, the mainly peasant population of the area found themselves saturated in the Nazi message uttered from the mouths of the highest leadership, including Hitler. The upshot was that the NSDAP gained nearly 40 percent of the votes in what Goebbels called 'the miracle of Lippe.' Those who hoped that the National Socialists' popularity would decline began to reverse that judgment.

After the result was known, Papen, surer than ever that Schleicher's days were numbered, began a fresh round of meetings with Hitler. At the second and most momentous of these at Dresden on 22 January, Oskar Hindenburg, the President's son was present. At some point during their discussion, Hitler asked to talk to him in private. It was during their hourlong tête-à-tête that the fate of Germany was sealed. It is widely believed that Hitler made an offer the young Hindenburg could not refuse: fresh investigations in the *Osthilfe* scandal, or support for Hitler's demands, which included the Chancellorship for himself. If he agreed to the latter course then he would be given more land plus army promotion.

In a taxi on the way back to their hotel an otherwise incommunicative Oskar Hindenburg commented to a companion that there was no help for it, 'the Nazis would have to be taken into the Government.' If a bargain had been struck that night the honoring of it began with the year when, in August 1933, 1000 tax free acres were added to the Hindenburg estates. A year later Oskar was promoted to major general.

On 28 January Schleicher bowed to the inevitable: there was no group within the Reichstag or outside it seriously prepared to make a deal with him. That day Hindenburg empowered his beloved Papen to begin negotiations to form a new government.

It was no more than a formality. Papen already had his government. It was true he had secured it only by sacrificing the Chancellorship. On the other hand, he would be Vice-Chancellor which, since the politically inexperienced Adolf Hitler would plainly find his position too onerous, really amounted to the same thing.

For the rest we are in the realm not just of German, but of world history. Within days the party, with Goering taking a leading part, began moving against its political enemies, particularly those of the Left, but the Reichstag fire on 27 February gave them the excuse to make these measures infinitely more comprehensive. It helped Hitler, too, with the passage of the Enabling Act on which his dictatorship was to rest.

On 5 March came the Reichstag election. Now the National Socialists had all the money they needed; the party ensured this by a deal with the richest and most influential entrepreneurs in the country. It also had access to all the media, including radio, from which it was previously barred. At the same time the SA and the SS freely disrupted meetings of other parties and terrorized those who attended them. For all this, the National Socialists received only 17,277,200 out of 39,343,300 votes cast, 43.9 percent. Other parties managed to increase their vote and even the Communists suffered comparatively small losses. At best Hitler had a bare majority, though it was helped by proscribing the Communists which prevented their deputies from taking their seats.

On 23 March, the Reichstag, meeting in temporary quarters in the Kroll Opera House, voted 441 to 94 in favor of Hitler's Enabling Bill. From now on he was free to rule entirely by decree, without more than formal reference to the President.

Already the process of *Gleichschaltung* or total coordination to National Socialism was well in hand: civil liberties had been suspended, the first concentration camps opened, Jews were being 'weeded out' of the professions and all positions of possible influence.

In August 1934 the only barrier between Hitler and unrestrained power fell: Hindenburg died. Within three hours Goebbels had announced the fusing of the two roles of Chancellor and President. The Führer of the NSDAP was now the Führer of Germany.

That year, too, had seen the Röhm purge in which every potential rival within the party and some outside had been summarily executed, including the head of the SA and Hitler's old associate, Ernst Röhm.

Hitler was now sure of his position. There followed the unilateral denunciation of the Treaty of Versailles. Germany, which had withdrawn from the League of Nations as early as October 1933, was now set on its course. This was to build it into a great military nation and the first step in this was the re-introduction of conscription.

The following year Hitler denounced another treaty, that which had turned the Rhineland into an unoccupied buffer zone between his own country and France. His excuse was the Franco-Soviet Pact. Against the advice of his more cautious associates, he ordered his army to march into the Rhineland.

During the Spanish Civil War, which started in 1936, he was able to find a testing ground for his forces and for the first time showed the world the nature of his regime. The world stood by impassively as it was to do for a further three years.

The subsequent years saw the annexation of Austria to the Third Reich, while the proclamation of the Nuremberg Laws which restricted German citizenship to 'Aryans' and the *Kristallnacht* with its government-orchestrated anti-Semitic riots, revealed the regime's intentions towards the Jews.

And all the time the control of government and party was being extended to cover every human activity. The nation which was without rival as the cultural center of Europe before 1933, had its creativity stifled under a blanket of state control and state philistinism. Progressive artists in all fields had to fall in with government *diktats* on taste or leave the country; if they happened also to be Jewish, they were denounced as 'degenerates' and went in danger of their lives. So complete was the supervision exercized that not even a landscape gardener could pursue his livelihood without permission.

As a substitute for what it had lost the German people were offered an unending military review – the stamp of feet and the shouts of the *Feldwebel*. The annual culmination of this was the great spectacular of the Nuremberg Rallies.

Still through the rest of the world no one moved. The Czechoslovak crisis came. And went after the British premier's meeting with Hitler. It took the invasion of Poland to bring the world, angrily, to its feet. It was, as we know, almost too late . . . .

Right: Hitler at his desk in the study at the Eagle's Nest, the Hofburg in Berchtesgaden.

9 November

The 9th of November was a national holiday in Nazi Germany. It was the date of the abortive Beer Hall Putsch in 1923. It was an opportunity for praise of the Nazis' struggle to attain power and an occasion to celebrate the achievements of Hitler's Reich.

Top left: Goering, Hitler and other veterans of the 1923 Putsch stand before Brown House in Munich in 1935.
Top center: A parade before the Temple of Honor in Munich's Königlicher Platz on 9 November 1935.
Top right: Hess, Himmler and Hitler at the Feldherrnhalle in 1934.
Above: The 10th anniversary of the Putsch in 1933 was led by the notorious anti-Semite Julius Streicher.

Hitler on Tour

Hitler traveled widely throughout Germany, particularly in the years before the war, and was one of the first of the world's political leaders to use planes to speed up his schedule. Later he traveled throughout Europe, first as an emissary, later as a conqueror.

Above: Hitler has a picnic lunch beside a road during one of his whirlwind tours across Germany.
Left: The Führer on a rail tour through Germany.
Below: Hitler's aide, Otto Günsche, helps a child give a bouquet to the Führer at the Brenner Pass on his way to Italy in 1938.
Top right: Hitler gives an autograph to a young admirer.
Topcenter: Hitler with Helga Goebbels in Bavaria.
Right: Hitler on the Rhine at Bad Godesberg.

Above: A German worker shakes the Führer's hand.
Right: Hitler leaves the hotel in Kleinkordbrünn-Friedrichrodd in June 1935. Nazi rallies hit their peak in the mid-1930s, but subsided as the war approached.

Above: Hitler pauses for a short read during an auto trip through Bavaria. His journeys through Germany ceased to be informal after 1933.

Above: Hitler with Hess at Wartburg Castle.
Right: Hitler leaves a Ju-52 transport of the Luftwaffe.

Hitler is greeted by a small crowd in Mainz.

Hitler The Artist

Hitler always had artistic tendencies which were allowed to wither after his years in Vienna before World War I. As an *artiste manqué* he founded an outlet in promoting patriotic art at the expense of 'decadent' or 'Jewish' art once he acquired power, and his grandiose schemes for the rebuilding of Berlin gave scope to his artistic temperament and imagination. Although most of schemes never got off the drawing board, a few of them, like the Olympic Stadium in Berlin, did. His relationship with Albert Speer, his principal architect, grew during those prewar years, and even during the war he planned to rebuild Germany once victory was achieved with Speer, who by 1943 had become his chief economics minister for war production.

Below: Speer and Hitler consult on a construction project.

Above: Hitler opens the Munich underground (subway) in 1938.
Below: Hitler lays a cornerstone in Nuremberg.

Above: Speer, Hitler and Ruft, another architect, plan the layout of the buildings in Nuremberg where future Party Days would be held.
Below: Hitler supervises the construction of the new Brown House in Munich, the party headquarters.

Above: A model at a professional architectural
construction exhibition in Berlin.

Above: Hitler and Bormann examine the plans for the rebuilding of Kassel.   *Above:* Model for the structure of a bridge in 1938.
Below: Goebbels, Hitler, Goering, Adolf Wagner and Hess on the Day of German Art in Munich.

Concentration Camps

Hitler was busy constructing other, less edifying buildings during the early years of the Reich. In his first year of power, 1933, several concentration camps were opened for political prisoners. Communists, anarchists, socialists as well as anyone actually or allegedly opposed to his regime were interned, to be joined later by Jews, gypsies and other 'undesirables.'

Top: The 'mess hall' at Dachau near Munich, 1933.
Above: The barracks for prisoners at Dachau.

Above: Goering and his fiancée enter the City Hall in Berlin for the civil ceremony prior to their church wedding.

Above: Mr and Mrs Goering leave the Berliner Dom after the religious ceremony.

Above: Hitler and Goering a few months before the wedding.

Above: The couple during the service held on 10 April 1935.

Above: The happy couple salute the crowds outside the Dom.

Above: Hitler greets the bridal couple in front of the Dom.

Goering's Wedding

Hermann Goering's first wife, Karin, died tragically and his remarriage in 1935 to film star Emmy Sonnemann was a major popular event in Berlin. Hitler was Goering's best man.

Above left: Hitler dressed in white tie and tails arrives at the Bayreuth music festival in 1938. Hitler loved the opera and Wagner in particular.
Above right: Hitler visits the Wagner Memorial in Leipzig in March 1934. Winifred Wagner stands next to Vice-Chancellor von Papen.
Below: Winifred Wagner, Hitler and Goebbels attend a ceremony commemorating Richard Wagner in Leipzig.
Right: Hitler at a performance of Richard Strauss' *Die Fledermaus* in 1937. Strauss left Germany in protest against the Nazi regime.

Hitler's Birthday

Hitler's birthday, 20 April, was always a holiday and an obvious occasion to emphasize Hitler's position as party leader, Chancellor and Führer as well as, in later years, supreme warlord. Never in human history has the cult of personality so enraptured a nation and its people.

Above: A young girl gives a grateful Führer a bunch of flowers on his birthday.

Right: Hitler reviews goosestepping SA men before the Chancellery on Berlin's Wilhelmstrasse on his birthday in 1935.

Above: Peasant women bring their presents to the Führer on his 46th birthday in 1935.

Above: Special decorations on the occasion of Hitler's 50th birthday in 1939.

Above: Propaganda blessing Hitler as the Kaiser was once blessed in the city of Worms.

Above: A variety of gifts were presented to the Führer to celebrate his birthday.

Hitler's SA and SS

Both the *Sturmabteilung* and the *Schützstaffeln* were special units for Hitler. Both began in the years of struggle long before Hitler ever had a hope of achieving power, and both units led the street fighting which helped add to the chaos which eventually brought him to the Chancellery.

Top left: Hitler and Hess salute an SA meeting in Weimar in 1936.
Bottom left: Hitler and Hess pose for a photograph with the *Gauleiters*.
Above: Ernst Röhm, Chief of Staff of the SA until he was murdered on Hitler's instructions, with other SA leaders.
Below: Heinrich Himmler and leaders of the SS in 1933.
Right: Hitler Youth, the SA and SS men of the future, on parade.

Above: SA, SS and *Stahlhelm* with Hitler at the Eagle's Nest in Berchtesgaden, Hitler's Bavarian retreat.
Below: Exhausted SA men after a long march on parade. At one time towards the end of the war 900,000 men reputedly served in the force.

Above: SA men listen intently to one of Hitler's speeches.
Above right: SA and SS on the march in Berlin in 1933.
Below right: Naval Hitler Youth at a rally for Hitler and *Gauleiter* Sprenger in Worms in 1935.

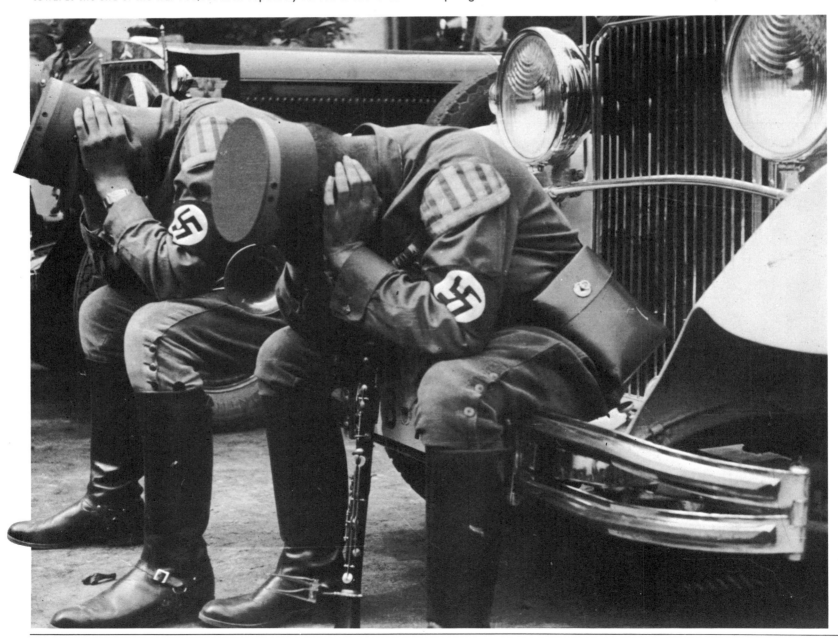

Above: Prussia's flags of glory wave at a ceremony held at the Tannenberg battlefield 27 August 1933.
Below: Hitler and Generals von Blomberg and von Fritsch review troops on Lüneburg Heath in September 1935.

Below: Generals von Fritsch, von Blomberg and Leitmann at the same exercise.

Above: Occasion marking Hitler's renunciation of the military restrictions of the Treaty of Versailles in 1935 in Berlin.
Below: Field Marshal von Mackensen, a war hero, supports the Führer.

Hitler and The Wehrmacht

The relationship between Hitler and his generals was a tenuous one before and throughout the war. Although they gave him grudging support, they did so with little enthusiasm, and Hitler always mistrusted his generals and their judgment.

Below: Generals von Blomberg, von Fritsch, Leitmann and Hitler on maneuvers in 1935.

Left: Generals Blaskowitz and von Brauchitsch on maneuvers with Hitler in the spring of 1936.
Above: Hitler reviews the troops in the closing parade of their exercises on Lüneberg Heath in 1935.

Below: Hitler and his generals at the funeral of Hans von Seeckt in 1936. Seeckt led the German Army during the 1920s. In attendance from left to right: von Rundstedt, Admiral Raeder, von Fritsch, Hitler, Goering, Field Marshal von Blomberg and von Heye.

Below: Generals von Fritsch, von Blomberg and Hitler at the 1935 military exercises. Both von Fritsch and von Blomberg were removed from office in 1938. Until that time von Fritsch had been commander of the German Army and von Blomberg had been War Minister.

Above: Hitler boards one of Germany's first U-Boats in Kiel. ·
Below: Aviso Grille, a training ship visited by Hitler in 1934.

Hitler and The Navy

The Kriegsmarine was limited drastically by the Treaty of Versailles, but after his coming to power Hitler proceeded to erase its restrictive clauses abetted by the British government which, knowing that it could not and would not enforce Versailles, concluded the Anglo-German naval pact with the Third Reich in 1935.

Above: A *Schnellboot* built for the German Navy in 1934.

Above: Hitler visits the *Schleswig-Holstein* in Hamburg's harbor.
Below: Goebbels, the Führer and Brückner visit the fleet in Kiel in 1933.

Above: Hitler aboard the cruiser *Leipzig* in 1934.
Below: Hitler reviews the crew of *Schleswig-Holstein*.

Far left top: Goering, Hitler and General Förster, commandant of the teaching division of the Luftwaffe, inspect new aircraft.
Left: These biplanes were the basis of the Luftwaffe in 1933. Modern technology soon replaced them.
Top: Hitler and von Blomberg at the launching of *Scharnhorst* in 1933, a project begun under the Weimar Republic.
Above: Hitler at the opening of Kiel Week in honor of the growing Kriegsmarine in 1936.
Below: Small boats attend the arrival of the fleet in Kiel in 1934.
Bottom inset: Hitler salutes the fleet in Kiel Week in 1936.

Hitler and The Church

Hitler's relationship with organized religion in Germany was tenuous during his first year in power. Since the Nazi Party had always been anti-establishment and anti-religious, Hitler and Goebbels flirted briefly with a revival of paganism based on the Nordic gods like Odin and Thor, but these plans were quickly dropped when public enthusiasm was not apparent. Hitler rushed to make his peace with the churches, especially the Catholic Church. The Concordat with the Papacy was signed in 1933. The Lutherans in the north were less enthusiastic, but toed the party line.

Right: Goebbels, Hitler and the Papal Nuncio Orsenigo meet the Berlin press.

Hitler attends the memorial service for the Polish dictator, Marshal Pilsudski, at Hedwigs Cathedral in Berlin in 1935.

Ein feierlicher Augenblick von der Grundsteinlegung zum Haus der deutschen Kunst.

Der päpstliche Nuntius Vasallo di Torregrossa spricht eben zum Führer:

„Ich habe Sie lange nicht verstanden.
Ich habe mich aber lange darum bemüht.
Heute versteh' ich Sie."

Auch jeder deutsche Katholik versteht heute Adolf Hitler und stimmt am 12. November
mit:

„Ja"!

Above: A monk who gave the benediction is greeted by SA men who held their anniversary celebration.
Left: Poster proclaiming Papist-Nazi solidarity quotes the Papal Nuncio, shown with Hitler, as saying, 'I have not understood you for a long time. But I have worried for a long time. Today I understand you.' The poster goes on to say that the public should vote for Hitler at the next election. There was no opposition party by that time.
Below: Outdoor mass is held in Munich in 1937 to bless the Nazi Party and the Führer.

Above: Hitler opens the first autobahn between Darmstadt and Frankfurt-am-Main in 1935.
Below: Hitler inspects construction work on the first autobahn near Frankfurt in September 1933.

Below: Hitler and a colleague dig the first spadefuls of earth on the day construction began for the autobahn.

The Autobahn

Hitler's most durable monument in Germany is the autobahn, begun during the Third Reich and of course expanded after the war and imitated throughout the world. Hitler took a keen interest in its construction as well as the Volkswagens which he planned for every German family. Few KdF-Wagens (Strength Through Joy) cars were built during the regime and its factories soon became war plants. Tanks, not cars was the automotive equivalent of guns.

Below: Part of the first autobahn.　　　　　　　　　　　*Below:* The first ride. *Below:* The Mangfall Bridge is built in 1935.

Volkswagen

The peoples' car, or Volkswagen, was created in 1934 as part of the Strength Through Joy movement. As every German family was meant to have one, German workers were encouraged to save five marks per week. Few were actually built.

Left: Hitler addresses the throng gathered at Wolfsburg for the opening of the Volkswagen factory.
Right: Hitler examines the interior of a new Opel at the Auto Show in Berlin in 1934.
Below: Hitler inspects the engine of a Mercedes in 1933.
Below right: Goering and Hitler admire a new convertible in 1934.
Bottom: Hitler checks out the legroom in the back seat of a new Volkswagen in 1938.

"It must be a greater honor to be a street-cleaner and citizen of this Reich than a king in a foreign state."

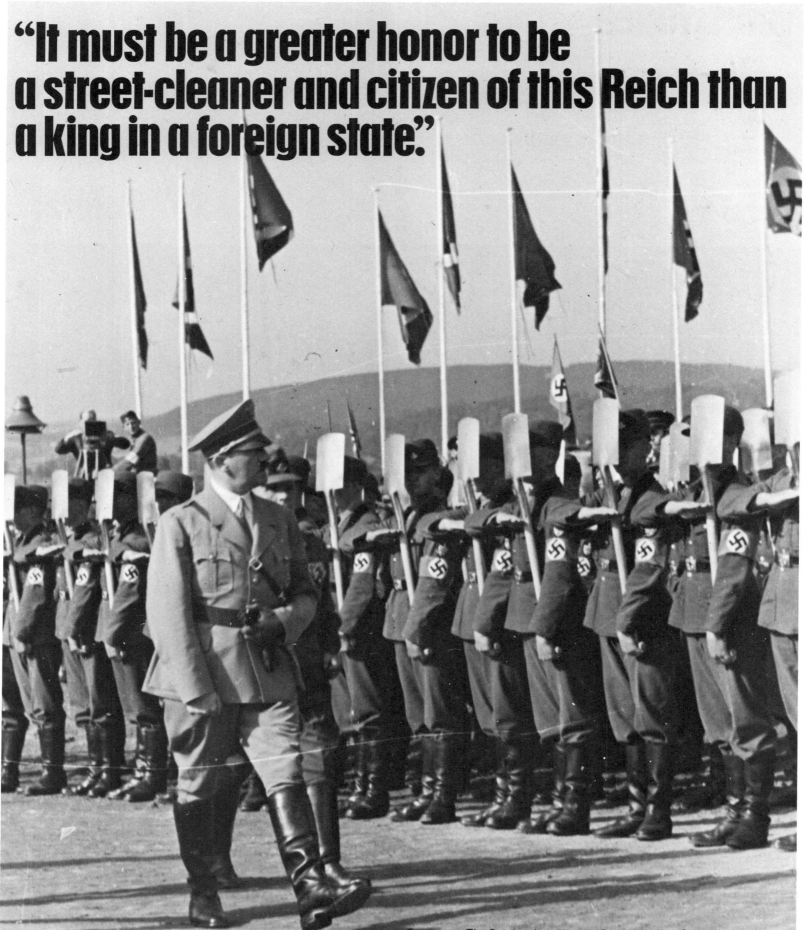

Above: Workers present spades at a rally for the Blood and Soil movement in Bückeburg in 1935.

Top center: The Reichsarbeitsdienst (German Labor Corps) before the symbol of their movement, *Blut und Boden* (Blood and Soil).
Top right: A squadron of 17 biplanes in formation over Bückeburg.
Center right: Hitler arrives at Bückeburg in 1934 for the Labor Corps rally.
Right: Opening ceremony of Green Week in 1934 honoring the Blood and Soil movement in Berlin before a famous portrait of the Führer.

Olympiad 1936

The 1936 Olympics were planned to be staged in Berlin during the Weimar period. Hitler used the games as a grand opportunity to show off his new order to the world and did so in grandiloquent style. The film Leni Riefenstahl made of the games was a classic. The power and magnificence of the Third Reich shone through it. Although Hitler was appalled when black athlete Jesse Owens of the USA won several events, he acted in a sportsmanlike manner generally, even permitting German Jews, deprived of many of their civil rights in the Nuremberg Laws of 1935, to participate in the games. The high summer of the Third Reich was 1936, and the Olympiad staged in Berlin was the first Olympiad to take on a political character. Sadly it was not the last to do so.

Left: Hitler and the Olympic Committee enter the stadium to open the games.
Below: Hitler officially opens the Olympiad.
Right: Hitler, Goebbels and Goering on the tribune salute the crowd which returns their greeting with a shout of Sieg Heil!

Hitler The Orator

As a speaker, Hitler was one of the most dynamic the world has ever known. Crowds were moved to ecstasy or tears within seconds. This is a series of photographs of one speech in Munich typical of thousands made during the Hitler Years.

Above: Hitler arrives at the hall as the band played the Badenweiler March, his signature melody for his arrival.

Above: Adolf Wagner salutes the Führer before he comes to the podium.

Above: Every speech began quietly, quickly rising to a crescendo.

Above: The expectant crowd awaits the arrival of the Führer.

Above: The pace quickens.

Above: The high point.

Above: The speech over, Hitler leaves the podium.

Above: Adolf Wagner thanks the Führer for his address.

Der Führer and Il Duce

The relationship between the German and Italian dictators became closer after 1935 when Anglo-French policy against Mussolini's Ethiopian invasion threw him into the arms of the Führer. Their meetings became more frequent until Italy was a client state of Germany by 1939.

Above: Hitler's first meeting with Mussolini in Venice in 1934. At this stage Hitler was a supplicant.

Above: Hitler returns from a state visit to Italy in 1938, by now the senior partner in the alliance.

Above: Hitler leaves Italy for Germany in 1938 as both dictators are saluted by Krause, Hitler's Shadow.

Above: Mussolini's visit to Berlin in 1937 was another of the increasingly frequent trips made by Il Duce to the Reich.

Above: Crowds cheering Il Duce on his visit to Munich in 1938 are restrained by the Deutschland Division.

Above: The cars of the dictators as they passed through Essen in the Ruhr industrial area.

Above: Hitler flanked by Mussolini's son-in-law, Count Ciano, and Goering on the balcony of the Reichschancellery.
Left: Hitler with Schaub, Bormann, Himmler and Krause behind in Munich after a speech.
Below: Goering, Hess, Mussolini and Hitler in Berlin in 1937.
Right: Mussolini greets Hitler for the first time in Venice in 1934. The picture leaves little doubt about who was the superior at the time.

The Pact of Steel

As Hitler and Mussolini grew closer, the Rome-Berlin Axis formed in 1936 was widened into the Pact of Steel which the two dictators signed in 1939. Italy was not, however, obliged to engage in any offensive war and therefore did not join Germany when World War II began with the invasion of Poland a few months later. Italy's intervention in June 1940 when France was all but defeated was not appreciated by the Führer.

Above: The band prepares for Hitler's disembarkation from the train from Italy at Munich station in 1938.

Above: Hitler is greeted by a variety of sycophants on the platform, 5 May 1938 just before the first Czech crisis which proved to be a false alarm.

Above: Hitler greeted by the Hitler Youth at the station. These formal occasions obliged anyone of even peripheral importance to make an appearance.

Above: Party members cheer the Führer on the platform. All trains had to be diverted to make way for the dictator's entourage and the ceremonies which always accompanied his arrivals and departures.

SS Leader Himmler and naval chief of staff Admiral
Raeder on a visit to Italy in 1937.
Below right: Hitler introduces Mussolini to Ritter von
Epp, a longtime Nazi supporter.

Above: Hitler greets Il Duce at Munich's railway station in 1937.
Right: A resplendent Mussolini and the Führer on the same occasion when they reviewed the troops.

Above: Goering, Count Ciano, Hitler and Mussolini at Munich station in 1938 during the first Czech crisis.

Above: Hitler in civilian mufti in Venice in 1934. On his first visit to Mussolini the Duce was not impressed by the Führer.

Hitler as Diplomatist

After the seizure of power the world wondered how radical Hitler's foreign policy was to be once he was firmly in office. The world did not have long to wait. Germany withdrew from the League of Nations, but despite her bellicose language, did not violate world peace in any other way once the putsch to overthrow the Austrian government proved abortive due to Mussolini's intervention.

Above: From left to right: Anthony Eden, John Simon, Dr Schmidt, the translator, von Neurath and von Ribbentrop discuss the Anglo-German naval pact of 1935 with Hitler.

Above: Hitler and Foreign Minister Constantin von Neurath, who was replaced by Ribbentrop in 1938, whose Büro Ribbentrop had already circumvented the Auswärtiges Amt.

Hitler made a valiant and successful attempt to win over the Papacy to at least tacit support of his regime, which he accomplished by support of the Catholic Church by the Nazi government.
Above: Hitler meets the Papal Nuncio to Germany with French Ambassador François-Poncet (left) after the 1933 Concordat with the Holy See.
Left: Hitler signs a document for his pilot, Flight Captain Bauer, before the Führer's favorite portrait of his hero, Frederick the Great of Prussia.
Below: The 1935 German Cabinet: from left to right, Dr Frank, Goebbels, Interior Minister Frick, Popitz, Cultural Minister Rust, Premier Goering, Kerrl, Foreign Minister von Neurath, Chancellor Hitler, Dr Lammers, War Minister von Blomberg, Economics Minister Dr Schacht, Justice Minister Dr Gürtner, Finance Minister von Schwerin-Krosigk, Darré, von Eltz-Rübenach, Labor Minister Seldte and State Secretary Funk.

Above: Japanese naval delegates are greeted by Hitler at the Wilhelmstrasse. Paper promises and pledges of mutual support by the Axis powers were never fulfilled.

Above: German Cabinet leaders in 1933. To the right of Goebbels and Hitler stand Goering, von Blomberg, Frick and von Neurath. Vice-Chancellor von Papen is second from right.

Above: Hitler explains his position to Sir Oswald Mosley (left), leader of the British Union of Fascists. Mosley's wife, Diana Mitford, and her sister Unity, accompanied him on his trips to Germany.

Above: Hitler with Foreign Minister Beck of Poland, with whom he signed a non-aggression pact in 1934. This pact's function was to counter an earlier Franco-Polish non-aggression pact.

Right: Hitler addresses a congress of the German Workers' Front in the Council of State.

Above: Members of the Reichstag listen to Hitler's speech explaining German foreign policy in May 1933 after the burning of the Reichstag building in February of that year.

Above: Hess and Hitler, Goebbels and von Papen (second row) at the first congress of the German Workers' Front in 1935. Von Papen became ambassador to Austria (1936–38) and Turkey (1939–44).

174

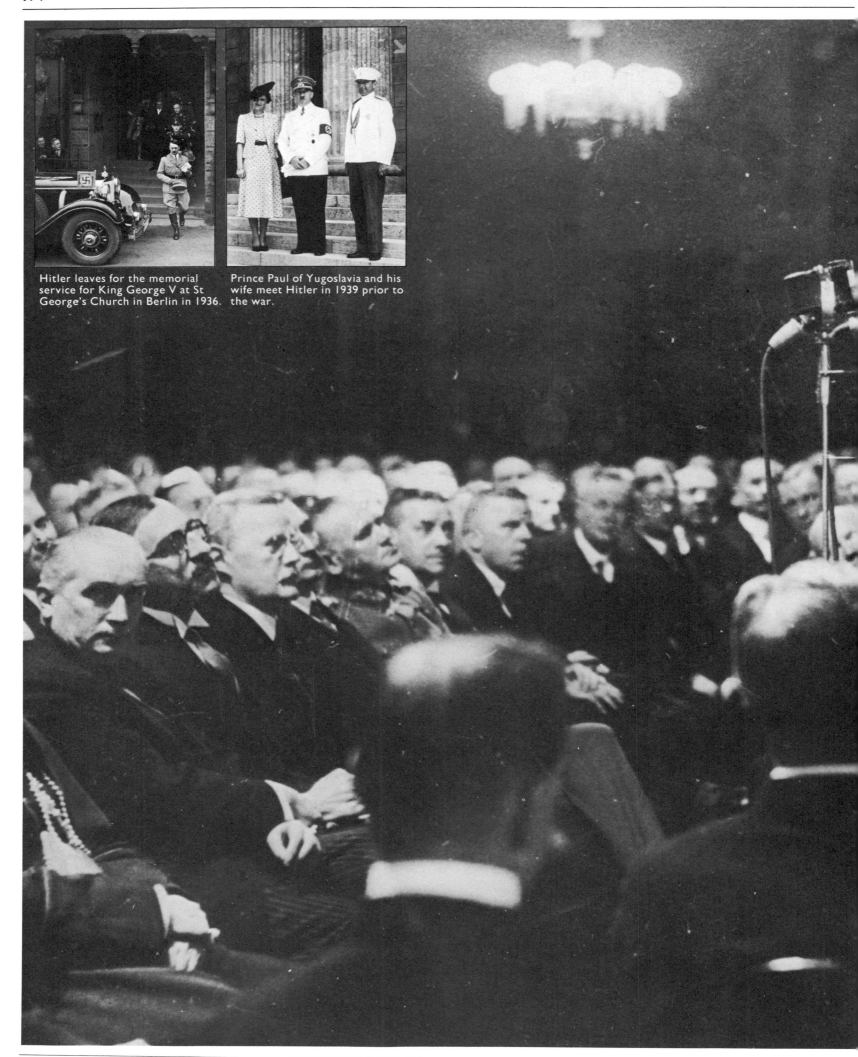

Hitler leaves for the memorial service for King George V at St George's Church in Berlin in 1936.

Prince Paul of Yugoslavia and his wife meet Hitler in 1939 prior to the war.

Below : Hitler addresses members of the foreign press in Berlin in 1933 to soothe their fears of his plans to redraw the map of Europe, fears which were eventually realized.

Bottom : Hitler greets English sportsmen and women in the Chancellery prior to the 1936 Olympics.

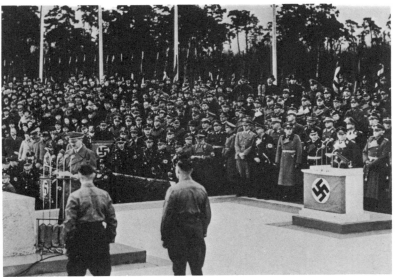

"An alliance whose aim does not embrace a plan for war is senseless and worthless."

Above: Hitler opens the German version of the National War College in 1937 as von Blomberg, Goering, Raeder, Beck, Schaub and Speer stand by.
Center top: Hitler and von Brauchitsch (right) at the 1938 Gross-Born maneuvers. At this time the generals were plotting Hitler's overthrow.
Far right top: Hitler meets with Generals von Rundstedt and von Brauchitsch prior to the 1938 maneuvers.
Far right center: Some early but obsolescent tanks on parade in 1933.
Below: Kempka, Hitler, Krause, Schmundt and Wiedemann attend the Gross-Born maneuvers in 1938.

Directive No. 1 for the Conduct of the War

1 Since the situation on Germany's Eastern frontier has become intolerable and all political possibilities of peaceful settlement have been exhausted, I have decided upon a *solution by force*.

2 The attack on Poland will be undertaken in accordance with the preparations made for 'Case White,' with such variations as may be necessitated by the build-up of the Army which is now virtually complete.

The allocation of tanks and the purpose of the operation remain unchanged.

Date of attack 1st September 1939.

This time also applies to operations at Gdynia, in the Bay of Danzig, and at the Dirschau bridge.

3 In the *West* it is important to leave the responsibility for opening hostilities unmistakably to England and France. Minor violations of the frontier will be dealt with, for the time being, purely as local incidents.

The assurances of neutrality given by us to Holland, Belgium, Luxembourg, and Switzerland are to be meticulously observed.

The Western frontier of Germany will not be crossed *by land* at any point without my explicit orders.

This applies also to all acts of warfare *at sea* or to acts which might be regarded as such.

The defensive activity of the *Air Force* will be *restricted* for the time being to the firm repulse of enemy air attacks on the frontiers of the Reich. In taking action against individual aircraft or small formations, care will be taken to respect the frontiers of neutral countries as far as possible. Only if considerable forces of French or British bombers are employed against German territory across neutral areas will the Air Force be permitted to go into defensive action over neutral soil.

It is particularly important that any infringement of the neutrality of other states by our Western enemies be immediately reported to the High Command of the Armed Forces.

4 Should England and France open hostilities against Germany, it will be the duty of the Armed Forces operating in the West, while conserving their strength as much as possible, to maintain conditions for the successful conclusion of operations against Poland. Within these limits enemy forces and war potential will be damaged as much as possible. The right to order *offensive* operations is reserved absolutely to me.

The *Army* will occupy the West Wall and will take steps to secure it from being outflanked in the north, through the violation by the Western powers of Belgium or Dutch territory. Should French forces invade Luxembourg the bridges on the frontier may be blown up.

The *Navy* will operate against merchant shipping, with England as the focal point. In order to increase the effect, the declaration of danger zones may be expected. The Naval High Command will report on the areas which it is desirable to classify as danger zones and on their extent. The text of a public declaration in this matter is to be drawn up in collaboration with the Foreign Office and to be submitted to me for approval through the High Command of the Armed Forces.

The Baltic Sea is to be secured against enemy intrusion. Commander-in-Chief Navy will decide whether the entrances to the Baltic should be mined for this purpose.

The *Air Force* is, first of all, to prevent action by the French and English Air Forces against the Germany Army and German territory.

In operations against England the task of the Air Force is to take measures to dislocate English imports, the armaments industry, and the transport of troops to France. Any favourable opportunity of an effective attack on concentrated units of the English Navy, particularly on battleships or aircraft carriers, will be exploited. The decision regarding attacks on London is reserved to me.

Attacks on the English homeland are to be prepared, bearing in mind that inconclusive results with insufficient forces are to be avoided in all circumstances.

signed: ADOLF HITLER

Above: General Sperrle speaks to two German flight officers at Santander airport in Spain during the Civil War.

Above: Franco (left) and Sperrle (right) outside Madrid during the final siege in 1939.

The Legion Condor

The Condor Legion was sent by Hitler to Spain to participate in the Spanish Civil War on the Nationalists' side. General Franco would never have been able to conquer the Republican forces without the massive aid which both Mussolini and Hitler provided. The return of the Condor Legion from Franco Spain after the collapse of the Republicans in March 1939 was a cause for general rejoicing throughout Germany.

Above: Ju-52s of the 57th Escadrille of the Condor Legion over Burgos. Their so-called atrocities in Spain were greatly exaggerated.

Above: Hitler attends the burial of 31 men who died aboard the ship *Deutschland* during its coastal action in the Spanish Civil War. The Nazi naval action in the Mediterranean off the Spanish coast discouraged active Franco-British support for the beleaguered Republic.

Hitler's support of the Condor Legion which aided Franco as well as his financial and diplomatic assistance to his fellow Fascist in Spain were immensely popular in Nazi Germany.
Above: Postcard commemorating the victory parade held in Madrid in 1939 to celebrate Franco's triumph.
Left: The burial service of the victims from the *Deutschland*.

Above: Postcard commemorating the return of the Condor Legion to Germany in May 1939. Hindenburg's portrait appears on the stamp.
Right: Returning troops from the Spanish Civil War are addressed by Goering in Berlin's Lustgarten.
Below: German sailors who fought in the Spanish Civil War celebrate their homecoming.
Center bottom: Spanish legionnaires at a dance celebrating their return in June 1939.
Extreme right: The Condor Legion parades in Berlin in June 1939.

"Neither western nor eastern orientation must be the future goal of our foreign policy, but an eastern policy in the sense of acquiring the necessary soil for our German people. Since for this we require strength, and since France, the mortal enemy of our nation, inexorably strangles us and robs us of our strength, we must take upon ourselves every sacrifice whose consequences are calculated to contribute to the annihilation of French efforts toward hegemony in Europe."

ГИТЛЕРосвободитель

Hitler as War Leader

In the first two years of World War II Hitler inspired the German people and many non-German sympathizers with the Nazi movement as much as ever. But when the war took a nasty turn for Germany in 1942, which soon led to collapse and disaster, Hitler became virtually a recluse, leaving most of the drum-thumping propaganda to Goebbels. Rather than Leader, Hitler became a totem, still idolized by millions, hated by millions more, but by 1943 always from a distance. His great speeches and rallies were over as time ran out on the Third Reich.

Left: A Russian poster praising Hitler as a liberator, useful in 1941 before Germany began her massive persecution of Slavs in the Ukraine and elsewhere.
Right: A wartime poster describing anyone who listened to foreign or clandestine radio broadcasts as a traitor.
Below: 'The Enemy Sees Your Light! Lights Out!' was the message on this wartime poster which was displayed widely after massive Allied air raids began.
Below right: Solidarity between the German worker and the soldier on the front is the theme of this poster.

Below: Hitler, Speer (far left) and high ranking officers on the Russian Front.
Bottom: Two posters showing the martyrdom of SA men fallen during street fighting in the Weimar years were displayed to inspire soldiers on the front to fight as their predecessors fought for Nazism.
Right: Hitler reviews a parade of armored cars in Berlin in 1940.

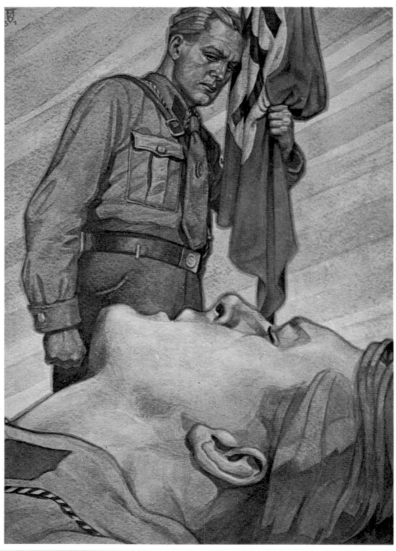

"What we must fight for is to safeguard the existence and reproduction of our race and our people, the sustenance of our children and the purity of our blood, the freedom and independence of the fatherland, so that our people may mature for the fulfillment of the mission allotted it by the creator of the universe."

Left: Poster glorifying the three armed services fighting together for the Third Reich.
Below: Jodl, Keitel and Hitler discuss strategy in April 1942.

"Loyalty, spirit of sacrifice, discretion are virtues that a great nation absolutely needs, and their cultivation and development in school are more important than some of the things which fill out our curriculums today."

Anschluss 1938

The seizure of Austria was swift and bloodless. Premier Schuschnigg was summoned to the Eagle's Nest in Berchtesgaden and told that Germany would take over Austria prior to the holding of the plebiscite over Austrian sovereignty. This was done in mid-March 1938 and the plebiscite showed a majority of Austrians in favor of the unification, probably a reflection of the Austrian national will. But with the plebiscite monitored by Nazi troops, no one will ever be sure.

Above: Hitler is greeted by his old teacher in Leonding when he entered Austria after the Anschluss.
Left: Hitler blesses an avid supporter during his triumphal parade through Austria.
Below: Hitler visits the cemetery where his parents were buried.

Above: Hitler in a pensive moment at his parents' grave.
It has been suggested that this was his first visit in decades, but it was politically useful to make a display of filial piety after Anschluss.

Above: Hitler after having visited his parents' grave.
The Führer made a great point of his Austrian origins once the Anschluss was completed.
Left: The church and cemetery where Hitler's parents were buried in Leonding.
Below: Hitler addresses a huge throng at the Hofburg in Vienna on 15 March 1938 after Anschluss.

The Munich Conference

As the Czech Crisis of September 1938 seemed to lead Europe inexorably toward war, Britain and France sought to appease Germany by relinquishing large sections of Czechoslovakia to the Third Reich against the Czech government's will and without prior consultation. The appeasement of Nazi demands only made war more certain on terms more disadvantageous to the Western Allies.

Above: Hitler makes a show of strength in a military parade at Breslau near the Czech frontier in July 1938.
Below: Mussolini and Rudolf Hess receive a guard of honor salute on their way to the Munich Conference. The Conference guaranteed Nazi control of Eastern Europe and permanent Western abandonment of the region.

Below: Chamberlain is greeted by General Keitel and Hitler in Hitler's mountain retreat in Bavaria during the Premier's first visit to Germany in September 1939.

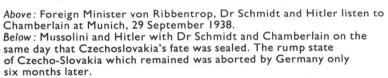

Above: Foreign Minister von Ribbentrop, Dr Schmidt and Hitler listen to Chamberlain at Munich, 29 September 1938.
Below: Mussolini and Hitler with Dr Schmidt and Chamberlain on the same day that Czechoslovakia's fate was sealed. The rump state of Czecho-Slovakia which remained was aborted by Germany only six months later.

Top: Mussolini signs the Munich Pact.
Above: Hitler signs the Pact as Ribbentrop watches. By this time Mussolini is in an animated discussion with Goering. The Munich Conference was Il Duce's last show of independent power. After 1938 he was dragged along by Germany on a path of conquest and destruction.

Left: Hitler is greeted by a German girl in the Sudetenland during the first week in October 1938 after the territory was occupied.
Above: Hitler with the Wehrmacht on the Schöber Line, the defensive barrier constructed by Czechoslovakia to counter a German invasion. It was taken without a shot being fired.
Below: Hitler is greeted in Brünn (Brno) on 15 March 1939 when Germany occupied the rest of Czechoslovakia. Many Czech cities had substantial German minorities which greeted Hitler warmly. The Czech majority felt otherwise.

Above: Hitler meets Dr Hacha, who replaced Premier Benes after his resignation following Munich. Hacha, in ill health, was greeted with full military honors and then was told that the rest of Czechoslovakia would be taken over within a few days. The frail old man collapsed and the rest of his country was seized by Germany in March 1939. Protectorates were established over Bohemia and Moravia under Reinhard Heidrich, the notorious SS officer, and Moravia became a German protectorate administered by a Catholic priest, Monsignor Josef Tiso. Tiso was tried after the war and was hanged on 3 December 1946.

Admiral Horthy Visits The Führer

Above: Berlin youth greet the arrival of the Hungarian dictator, Admiral Nicholas Horthy.
Right: Horthy is shown the construction plans for the Luitpoldhalle in Nuremberg to be used for future rallies.
Below: Hitler and Horthy (partly obscured) visit Heligoland during the Regent's visit in 1938.
Below right: Horthy and Hitler are saluted by an armed guard outside Berlin's railway station upon his arrival.

Below: Frau Horthy launches the new German battlecruiser *Prinz Eugen* at Kiel during the state visit.
Bottom: Admiral and Frau Horthy salute the launching of the *Prinz Eugen* as it pulls out of the slips.

Horthy was given a big parade with full military honors during his visit in 1938.

Above: Hitler and Horthy pass by columns of troops during the parade on 25 August.
Above right: German artillery passes by the reviewing stand with Hitler and Horthy in the foreground.
Right: Hitler escorts Frau Horthy into the party held in her husband's honor at Charlottenburg Castle.
Below: Over 16,000 Wehrmacht troops paraded before the Hungarian leader.

The Conquest of Poland

Hitler's invasion of Poland on 1 September 1939 began the Second World War, but the overrunning of Germany's eastern neighbor took only four weeks. The heaviest fighting occurred during the defense of Warsaw, in which the Poles fought valiantly in a hopeless cause. The Soviet Union moved into eastern Poland on 17 September to claim their share.

Above: Hitler salutes a tank officer during the Polish campaign.
Left: An heroic portrait of the Führer as war leader.
Below: Members of Hitler's personal staff on the Polish front.
Bottom: Hitler and Bormann (to Hitler's right) on a bridge in Danzig, taken on the first day of the Polish campaign. The Shadow, Krause, stands at the far right.
Right: Hitler's car and entourage are greeted rapturously by citizens of Danzig after its seizure in September 1939.
Danzig was administered by the League of Nations until its seizure, but was almost 100% German-speaking, and most were pro-Nazi, including the Mayor of the Hanseatic city.

Above: Hitler watches as German infantry and artillery move in for the siege of Warsaw on 21 September 1939. By this time most of Poland had been overrun.

Below: A painting of Hitler in Poland by Konrad Hommel. Although Keitel and Goering were shown along with other Nazi leaders, the juxtapositioning of the entire group was entirely fanciful.

Above: Hitler views the sights in Warsaw after its capture.
Below: Hitler is saluted in Poland as Martin Bormann follows closely behind him.

Below: Hitler addresses his troops in Poland after its conquest.
Bottom: Goering, Bodenschatz, Keitel, Hitler and von Ribbentrop study a map of Poland during the campaign.

Above: The Führer consoles a wounded veteran in 1940.
Below: Hitler confers with his adjutant Schmundt during the 1940 campaign at Hitler's headquarters.

Above: Hitler enjoys his Christmas dinner with a Wehrmacht regiment.

Above: Hitler with paratroops after their capture of Fort Eben-Emael in Belgium in May 1940.
Below: Hitler with Ernst Udet, the World War I pilot who shot himself the following year, and Schaub (left) with Goering and Bormann (right) at the Führer's headquarters in Belgium in May 1940.

Above: The Führer is driven to his new Belgian headquarters near Bastogne on 16 May 1940, only six days after the Blitzkrieg had begun.
Below: Hitler poses with the paratroops who captured Fort Eban-Emael in their famous attack using gliders.

The Fall of France

The complete collapse of the Western Front in a space of six weeks was as astounding to Hitler as it was to his opponents. The French Army, excluding the British Expeditionary Force which aided it, was larger than Germany's on paper, but superior German tactics as well as a collapse of French morale hastened the debacle. Hitler ordered that the surrender take place at Compiègne in the same railway carriage in which Germany's capitulation to France in 1918 took place. The French humiliation was complete.

Left: Graves of five Wehrmacht soldiers on a French field where they fell during the 1940 campaign.
Extreme left top: Hitler and his staff flanked by Albert Speer (left of Hitler) in Paris after the fall of France.
Top left of center: Hitler and his entourage wait to greet Mussolini's arrival in Munich on 18 June 1940. Hitler was surprised and appalled when Mussolini invaded France on 10 June after the battle of France was won. Italian troops fought badly however, and Hitler refused to invite Mussolini to the surrender ceremony in Compiègne.
Top right of center: Hitler greets some of the combatants in France upon their arrival in Munich in June 1940.
Above: Hitler and Mussolini in Munich on 18 June.

Far left top: Hitler and Mussolini enter Hitler's office in Munich for their 18 June talks in 1940.
Left center top: The inside of the Führer Building where they met.
Left: Hats of the two dictators on the ledge outside the office in which they met.
Below left: Von Brauchitsch, Raeder, Hitler, Hess, Goering and von Ribbentrop followed by Schmündt and Brückner in the forest of Compiègne prior to the French surrender.
Below: Vice Admiral LeLuc, General Bergeret, General Hüntziger and M Noel, the French plenipotentiaries, leave the railway car in Compiègne after having signed the capitulation.
Bottom: The famous railway carriage in which the truces of 1918 and 1940 were signed on the quiet morning before the surrender.

The Victory Parade

The parade held by Hitler to honor those who fought in the victorious battle in the West in May–June 1940 was the most glorious day for German arms in history. It was more than a celebration of a victorious campaign It was as if the war were over and Germany had won it. But the war had only begun by July 1940. Hitler reached his pinnacle of power on the day of the victory parade in Berlin.

Above: Wehrmacht troops carrying their battle flags goosestep past Hitler in the victory parade.

Below: Artillery and infantry march along the parade route.

Above: Wehrmacht troops bedecked with flowers celebrate the triumph.

Above: A machine gun is covered with flowers and its gunner admired by German girls along the parade route.
Below: SA, SS and Berlin police try vainly to restrain the Berlin throng on victory day. The victory celebrations of 1940 assumed that the war was all but over. It had only just begun.

Above: Boy with camera seeks a better view of the parade atop the statue of Frederick William I in Berlin.
Below: German police and soldiers try to restrain the enthusiastic throng. It is remarkable that Hitler needed little police protection. He usually disdained caution even in the matter of his own personal security, but he would have made a very easy target for any would-be sniper or assassin in the crowd.

Above: Child wearing a Luftwaffe cap at the parade.
Right: The big moment; the Führer passes with the road carpeted by flowers.
Below: It was not all spontaneous. Girls strew flowers along Hitler's path hours before his arrival. Tens of thousands of flowers covered the path of the entire parade route and thousands more were thrown by the crowds.

218

Mending Fences

After the conquest of France Hitler tried to cement old relationships and establish new ones with real or would-be allies in the fight against Britain and later the Soviet Union. Finland had its fingers burned in their war with Russia in 1939–40, but nevertheless was eager to recover lost territory. Franco's Spain, however, had just lost over 10% of its population in the Civil War and refused to join the Axis formally, although remaining friendly to its fellow-fascist states.

Above: Hitler greets Franco on the Franco-Spanish border at Biarritz to convince him to join the Axis. He failed.

Below: Hitler addresses the Reichstag in July 1940 after the fall of France proclaiming Germany's hegemony in Europe.

Above: Hitler congratulated General Mannerheim of Finland on his 75th birthday. Finland fought with Germany against Russia 1941–44.

Above: Hitler addresses a gathering in Berlin's Sportpalast in 1941 prior to the invasion of Russia. The banner reads 'With Our Banners is Victory!'

Above: Hitler and Martin Bormann (far right) in Austria, 1941.
Below: An Austrian enthusiast listens to his Führer.

Above: General Count von Schulenberg's bier is saluted by Hitler.
Below: Field Marshal Keitel briefs Hitler on the position in Russia in July 1941. Keitel was nicknamed 'Lakeitel' (lackey) because of his sycophancy to Hitler.

Below: Rosenberg and Lammers, responsible for resettlement of civilians on the Eastern Front, discuss their policy with Hitler. Resettlement usually meant recruitment for slave labor or concentration camps for thousands of people of several nationalities.

Above: Hitler is greeted by Berlin children and their mothers on his birthday, 20 April 1942.

Above: Keitel, Hitler and von Leeb study a Russian map during the first months of Operation Barbarossa.

Below: Hitler reviews his troops in Russia.

Disaster in Russia

From 1942 onwards, after the string of German victories came to a halt, Hitler's public appearances before his troops or civilians became less frequent and more subdued. Hitler's whole regime lived on victories. Once these became fewer and finally ceased, enthusiasm for the Nazis turned to resignation and a determination by the German people to defend their country against the invaders who were closing the net around them.

Below: King Boris of Bulgaria visits Hitler on the Eastern Front in 1943. Bulgaria left the war just over a year later.

Above: Hitler meets Count Ciano in the company of General Jodl (right) and interpreter Schmidt in 1942.

Above: A German girl congratulates Hitler on his birthday in 1942 near the Wolf's Lair, his headquarters in East Prussia.

Above: King Boris speaks to Hitler's pilot, Bauer, during his visit to the Eastern Front in 1943.

The Long Retreat

After the loss of the Battle of Kursk in July 1943, Germany's hopes of ultimate victory in the war faded with each passing day. Hitler watched the long retreat on the Eastern Front and in Italy with growing concern, and spent more and more of his time in the Wolf's Lair in East Prussia, hoping for some miracle which he knew in his heart of hearts would never come.

Top left: Goering, Hitler and Speer in the Wolf's Lair in the summer of 1943.
Left: The Turkish delegation visits Hitler in East Prussia in 1943. Turkey remained a benevolent neutral to Germany during the war but their role became less important as the Wehrmacht began to withdraw from Russia.
Above: Officers of the Leibstandarte Adolf Hitler Division of the SS visit the Wolf's Lair in 1944.
Right: Hitler visits an armaments factory on the occasion of his birthday in April 1943.

Below: The long retreat begins in the winter of 1943.

Below: Russian tanks press their attack forward as the Wehrmacht is pushed inexorably toward Berlin.

Below: Hitler congratulates Baldur von Schirach, former Hitler Youth leader, on his conduct in Vienna at the Wolf's Lair in October 1943. Bormann stands at the right. By this time Bormann shielded the Führer from the rest of his staff.

Below: Hitler somberly shakes the hand of a supporter in late April 1944. Hitler's public appearances were increasingly rare during the latter stages of the war, and stopped almost completely after the Bomb Plot of July 1944.

Below: Hitler in a forlorn mood meets Gauleiter Giesler as Martin Bormann, who dominated Hitler's life by 1944, lurks in the background.
Right: SS Chief Himmler confers with Hitler in October 1944.

Above: Hitler feeds a little fawn near the Berghof, one of Hitler's many retreats.
Below: Hitler and some local children. Baldur von Schirach on the right.

Above: Goering, von Blomberg and Hitler at the retreat.
Below: Hitler takes a winter stroll near the Berghof.
Right: A lucky admirer gets the Führer's autograph.

Berchtesgaden

Hitler's retreat in the mountains of Obersalzburg in Berchtesgaden near the Austrian-Bavarian border was a beautiful complex. Hitler lived in a simple house, protected by hundreds of armed guards in barracks located near the hideaway. Its pastoral beauty and serene atmosphere in the wooded Bavarian Alps revitalized him. Eva Braun spent most of her time in Berchtesgaden, hidden from public eye.

The coming to power of Hitler and the National Socialists in January 1933 was by no means the great shock story, or even the principal story of that year to most Americans. Roosevelt's assumption of the American presidency some five weeks later had a far greater and more immediate impact. Banks were closing all over America. Eighteen million people, representing about 40 percent of the work force, were unemployed. Soup kitchens abounded. Mortgages were being foreclosed. Dust storms were turning once productive farms into deserts. Men and businesses were going bankrupt. Even some State governments (such as Michigan's), ran out of money and were forced to pay their employees in scrip rather than cash. The United States and its economy, once considered the richest and most invulnerable in the world to crisis and breakdown, were rapidly grinding to a halt. Barter, black market and

breadline made President Herbert Hoover's claims of 'prosperity just around the corner' sound hollow and callous. Like the Germans, facing a similar and not unrelated crisis, most Americans looked to their new leader for guidance and decision. Fear of Hitler, a common phenomenon among many Germans, some Europeans and all Jews, was unknown in the United States in 1933. Fear of poverty, fear of the future and fear of unemployment in an age without social security, government old age pensions, national health insurance or unemployment compensation was rife. And like the Germans, the Americans found guidance and decision in President Roosevelt, as the Germans found Hitler to be a decision maker without parallel.

This is far from saying that the decisions these two leaders took were similar at most levels. But where Hitler had his *Gleichschaltung*, Roosevelt had his TVA, NRA, AAA, WPA,

Below: Hitler addresses thousands in Berlin's Lustgarten on 1 May 1934 and millions over the radio after his consolidation of power.

The Greater Reich:

An American View

which hoped to relieve the ill-effects of the world's economic depression and the ravages of unemployment. Most historians would agree today that some of FDR's projects worked. Many others did not. There were still almost ten million unemployed at the end of his first year of administration. But in the realm of relieving bad housing, unemployment and despair for most of his people, Hitler was an unparalleled success. By 1935 there were no unemployed in Germany. Roads were built. Industries revived even without the assistance of government-supported war industries in the first Hitler years. Housing projects, cheap holidays subsidized by the government and the ending of poverty were still an American goal long after they were achieved in Germany. And as a result most Americans turned their backs on Europe and the rest of the world in an attempt to conquer their own problems at home.

Hitler addresses a throng gathered at Tempelhof Field in Berlin on 1 May 1934 to commemorate the festival of German Workers.

The Final Years

Hitler spent his last two years in three locations: the Berghof in Berchtesgaden with Eva Braun, the Wolfsschanze in Rastenburg, East Prussia, and the Reichschancellery in Berlin. Hitler and his wife, whom he married hours before they committed suicide, died in the Bunker beneath the Chancellery in the Wilhelmstrasse. Visited by his generals and cosseted from outside influences by Speer and Bormann, Hitler was an increasingly haunted and lonely man in his final years, particularly after the Bomb Plot of 20 July 1944, tortured by the knowledge that his cause was lost and grasping at straws when the odd piece of favorable information filtered through to him in the form of exaggeration and flattery.

Top: Hitler greets Mussolini in one of Il Duce's increasingly frequent visits to Rastenburg.
Left: General Schörner and Hitler study a map in the company of a group of disheartened officers in 1944.

Four views of the Berghof, in Berchtesgaden. *Above:* The breakfast room. *Below:* Hitler on the terrace with some locals.

Above: The living room. *Below:* The exterior of the house in 1932 when Hitler was visited by some enthusiastic local girls.

The Berghof, Hitler's Alpine retreat in Berchtesgaden.

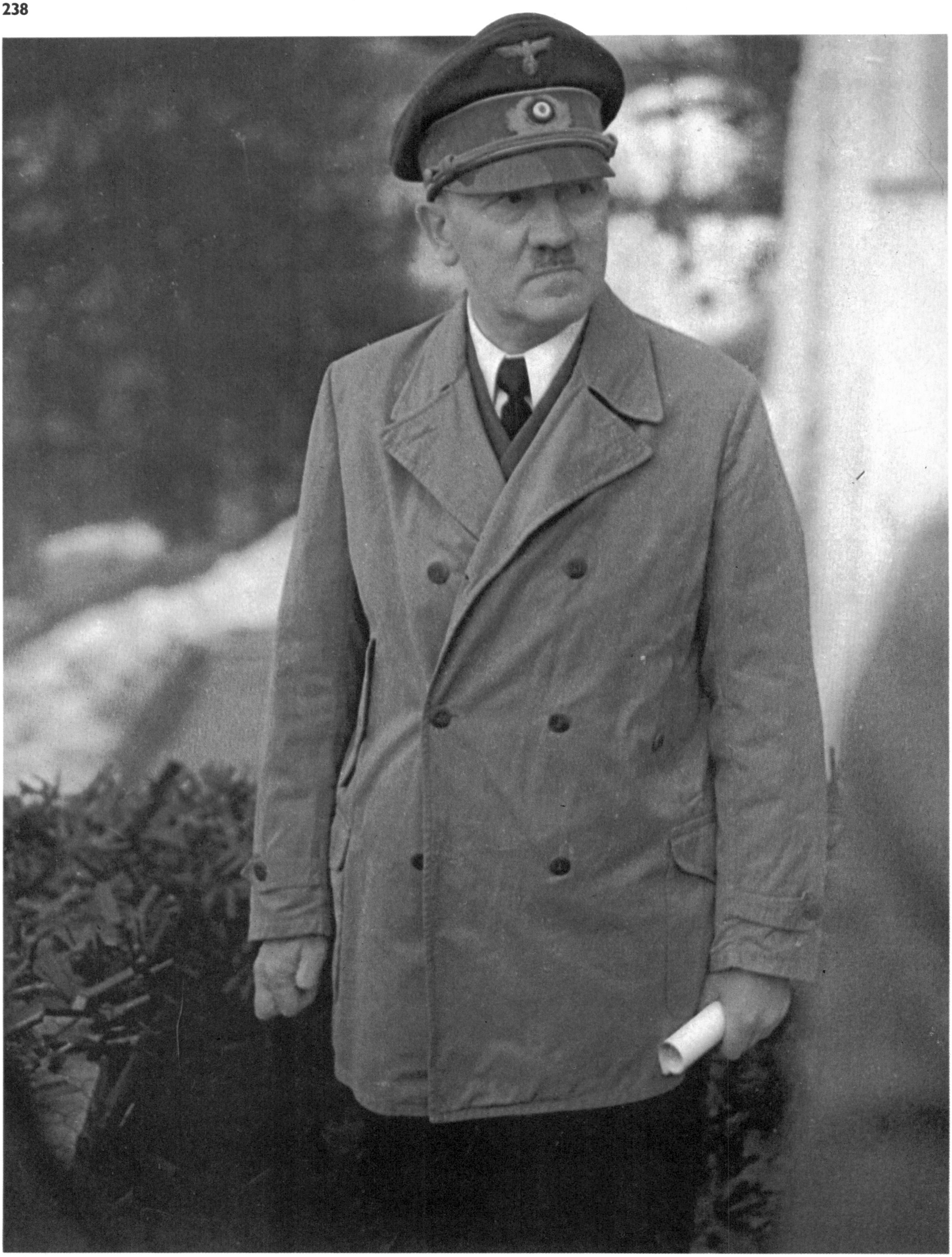

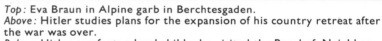

Left: A forlorn Hitler leaves the Wolf's Lair, his headquarters in Rastenburg, East Prussia for the last time early in 1945.
Top: Eva Braun gathering flowers near the Berghof.
Above: Hitler and his secretary at the Berghof.
Below: Hitler and his faithful Alsatian, Blondie.

Top: Eva Braun in Alpine garb in Berchtesgaden.
Above: Hitler studies plans for the expansion of his country retreat after the war was over.
Below: Hitler comforts a local child who visited the Berghof. Neighborhood children were welcomed at the Eagle's Nest.

Above: The ruins of the Berghof after its capture by the Americans at the end of the war.
Left: One of the last wartime portraits of Hitler.

"I must not measure the speech of a statesman to his people by the impression which it leaves in a university professor, but by the effect it exerts on the people."

Above: An enthusiastic jubilant crowd composed of people from all age groups and classes welcomes Hitler to Buckeburg for a rally in 1935. The Bückeburg rally was a triumph of volkish ideology, where tens of thousands of Germans in peasant costume paraded their traditional dress before the admiring eyes of their Führer.

In Britain, where the Depression bit less dramatically and deeply simply because there had been no effective post-World War I recovery in the first place, the Liberal and Labour parties fixed their attentions on domestic matters. The Conservatives, who held effective power throughout the 1930s, tended to welcome Germany's economic recovery under Hitler as a new opportunity in a foreign market close to home. Though most Britons, like most Americans, considered the Nazi regime to be somewhat distasteful and sordid, particularly in the context of its blatant racism and anti-Semitism, they did not think about it much. Those who did, apart from British and American Jews, to a greater or lesser degree admired Hitler's swift and remarkable achievements in the German economic sphere, and there were even those who argued that Britain and America ought to emulate Hitler's deeds. After all, Hitler claimed to be a socialist, albeit of a certain type which rejected international socialism in favor of national socialism in one country. Therefore, Left Wing socialists and Communists disagreed violently with Hitler's ideological stance, but could not have found too much wrong in what he did specifically on the economic front, since they were proposing similar measures. And of course, there were Right Wing imitators of Hitler's style both in Britain and America who found little or nothing wrong in whatever Hitler was doing, such as Sir Oswald Mosley's British Union of Fascists, and the far less successful American fringe group, Fritz Kuhn's German-American Bund which held Nazi rallies in Madison Square Garden to packed houses and which baited the Jews with equal vociferousness but with less violence than Mosley's bully-boys in London's East End.

Hitler, always subliminally conscious of the effect of his movement and its ideas, was aware of the shameful fact that many if not most of the northwest Europeans, Americans, Canadians, Australians and South Africans shared his racial prejudices. Hitler, Goebbels and the rest bellowed the principles of racial hatred and anti-Semitism that were merely whispered and joked about in country clubs, college fraternities and fashionable soirées in the Anglo-American world. It was therefore not what Hitler said but the way he said it that tended to pall. Such vehemence in the early 1930s would be attributed to 'continental emotionalism' by those who ought to have known better. Though few would have condoned concentration camps, the elimination of opposition political parties and the virtual abolition of freedom of speech, press and assembly in Germany, anti-Semitism, which lay at the heart of Hitler's philosophy, was as American as apple pie and as British as steak and kidney pudding. Americans and Australians had adopted policies towards immigrants from Asia, Africa, southern and eastern Europe which Hitler would have been proud of long before National Socialism was ever a threat to world security. The Ku Klux Klan, after all, was an American phenomenon. Even a cursory reading of British authors such as H Rider Haggard, Somerset Maugham, Evelyn Waugh and G K Chesterton would soon expose a subdued, gentlemanly sort of racism in Britain which was consonant with institutions as hallowed as the *Boys' Own Newspaper* and the British Empire itself, which controlled about a quarter of

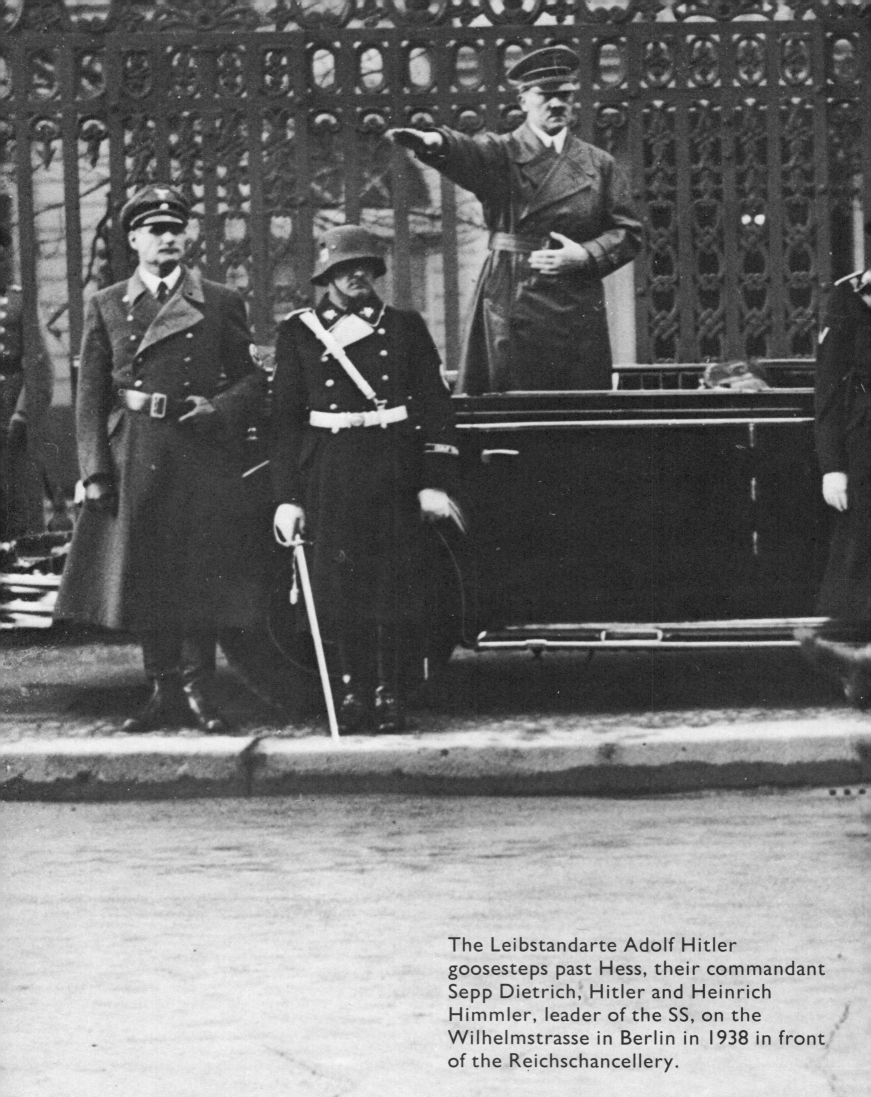

The Leibstandarte Adolf Hitler goosesteps past Hess, their commandant Sepp Dietrich, Hitler and Heinrich Himmler, leader of the SS, on the Wilhelmstrasse in Berlin in 1938 in front of the Reichschancellery.

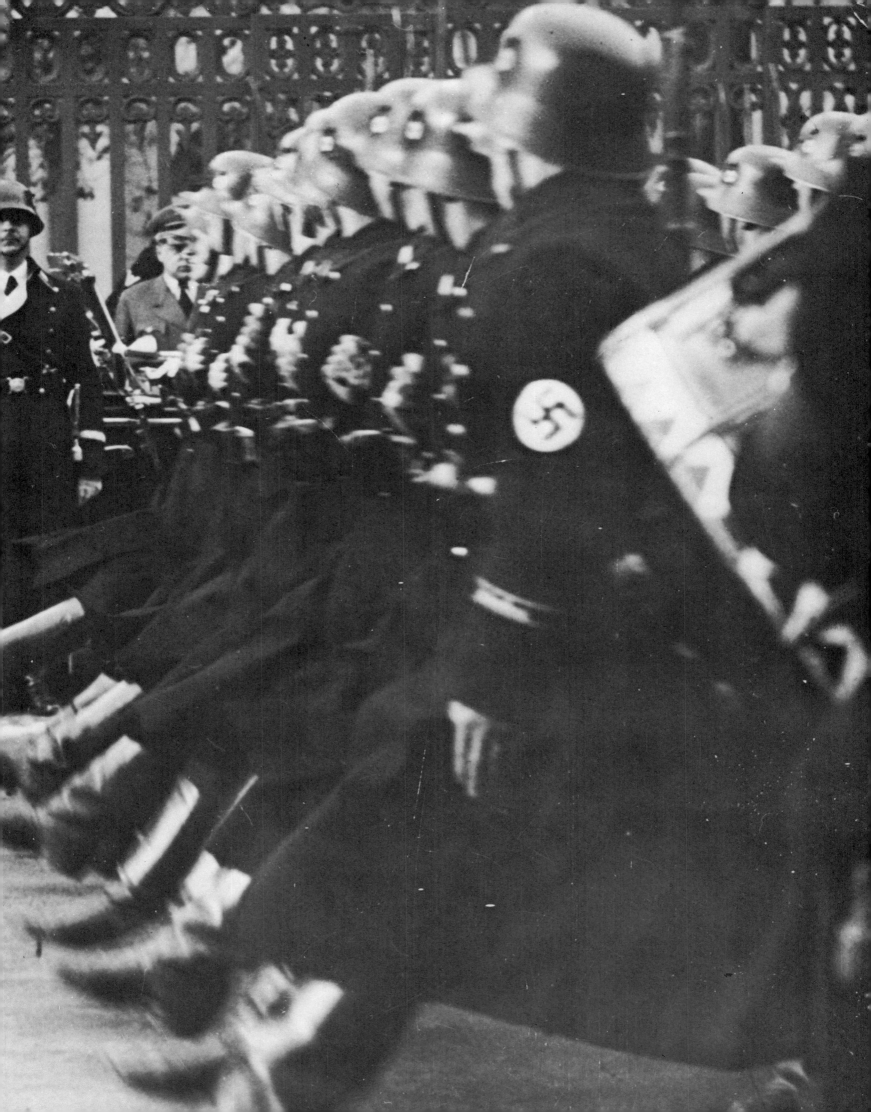

the world's population, most of them non-white. Imperial policy, as expressed in the White Papers on Palestine in 1922 and 1939, even limited the emigration of Jewish refugees from the Nazi regime to what Lord Balfour had once described as the 'Jewish national homeland,' then ruled by Britain under a League of Nations mandate. In short Hitler was expressing in a coarse manner, sentiment which Germans shared with Britons and Americans alike.

Grudging admiration for Hitler's economic achievements and a quiet disregard of his achievements of a more unsavory nature in the Anglo-American world allowed Hitler to build the basis of a war machine in Germany during his first three years in power without much critical comment from those who mattered in either London or Washington. Britain co-operated with Hitler in rewriting the Treaty of Versailles by negotiating the Anglo-German naval pact in 1935. Both Britain and America failed to effectively discourage Mussolini's Abyssinian adventure and only succeeded in driving him into Hitler's camp when the Rome-Berlin Axis was formed in 1936. The Anglophone powers turned a blind eye to the support that Hitler and Mussolini gave to Franco's Falangist coup in Spain. And when Wehrmacht troops poured into the Rhineland in March 1936, France was unable to gain Britain's cooperation in stopping this open violation of the Versailles Treaty, even though it is now clear that Hitler would have ordered an immediate retreat if any opposition had been shown by either France or Britain. Those two powers, the only ones capable of stemming Nazi expansion in Europe, simply had lost faith in the treaties they had drawn up at the end of World War I.

The United States was equally disillusioned by the experience of the last world war. A Congressional investigation under the leadership of Gerald Nye, carried out in 1934–35, blamed the American entry into the war as a conspiracy of Wall Street bankers and industrialists. The various neutrality acts passed by Congress from 1935 onward on an annual basis indicated the degree to which isolationism gripped the American political conscience. Even when Roosevelt, in his first attempt to break the political climate, alluded to the Axis powers in his speech in Chicago in October 1937 when he suggested, without naming names, that the world's aggressors should be 'quarantined,' the outcry against his rather mild statement from all quarters from Tribune Tower to Times Square forced him to realize that it would take more than words to break the disillusionment with 'foreign entanglements' which most Americans felt to be the legacy of World War I.

Britain and France, who had fought longer and sacrificed forty or fifty times more men on the battlefields of Europe between 1914 and 1918, were disillusioned in another and perhaps more fundamental way. They could not face up to the fact that when Hitler threatened their own security, as by 1937 he quite clearly intended to do, they would have to sacrifice yet another generation of their youth to the mouth of the cannon to prevent it. Although lone figures like Churchill and de Gaulle, as yet ignored and unheeded, had warned against Hitler's long-term intentions in Europe, those in positions of power flinched from the challenge. Although by 1936 Britain had already begun to build the nucleus of a modern air force and the US had surreptitiously begun a reconstruction of the American fleet, under Roosevelt's guidance, leaders of every political stripe refused to warn their populations of the struggle which lay ahead for fear of risking unpopularity. This was as true of Baldwin and Chamberlain as it was of George Lansbury of the Labour Party. Indeed, Labour steadfastly opposed defense expenditures, and in the United States, the Republicans led the isolationist cause. There were few, in or out of government, who would face up to Hitler's challenge

to the postwar *status quo* in what was, by 1937, palpably a prewar era. But for the United States, there was a difference, and an important one. Most Americans perceived the challenge Hitler was making to the *European status quo* as not their problem. A generation before they became convinced that Germany was out to conquer the world. It subsequently became clear that even the grandiloquent Kaiser had nothing so elaborate in mind, and the postwar settlement had indicated that rather than making the world safe for democracy, as Woodrow Wilson had hoped, the Americans had helped make the world safe for the British and French empires, which had expanded dramatically at the end of the war at the expense of the defeated Central Powers. Most Americans were simply unwilling to sacrifice either blood or treasure for the Western Allies a second time. So, while Britain and France were changing their view of Hitler because he was clearly a challenge to their interests, it was for that very reason that the Americans were not prepared to support those interests. Only when and if the interests of the United States were threatened would the Americans be willing to go to war once more.

This point was not lost on Hitler. Nor was it lost on Daladier and Chamberlain, when first they condoned Hitler's seizure of Austria in the spring of 1938, and then collaborated with him to partition Czechoslovakia at the Munich Conference in the autumn. Hitler's audacity was encouraged by American isolationism and Britain's fear of war. This fear was heightened by Chamberlain's realization that he risked Imperial solidarity if Britain decided to go to war over the Sudetenland in 1938. Canada, Australia and South Africa would not have fought with Britain, for if Chamberlain characterized Czechoslovakia as 'a farway country about which we know nothing,' Prague was even further away from Canberra, Pretoria and Ottawa than it was from London. Only New Zealand among the Dominions was loyally prepared to follow Whitehall's decisions whatever they were. Britain's only hope was to turn Hitler's attentions toward eastern Europe, and only to oppose him actively if he challenged the neutrals in the Low Countries and Scandinavia or the Maginot Line. Thus, when in 1939 Hitler seized what was left of Czechoslovakia, plucked Memel from Lithuania and threatened Danzig and the Polish Corridor, Britain and France talked with each other and Warsaw, made military preparations, but did not take active steps to stop Hitler's further conquests.

They should have looked to their natural ally in the east, Stalin's Soviet Union, for support if they were serious about preventing Poland from falling into Nazi hands. But although talks began at arms' length, both Stalin and Hitler realized that as Soviet aid offered in the Czech crisis had been ignored, the Western Allies were unlikely to contemplate a meaningful alliance with Russia. Therefore Hitler and Stalin signed Poland's death warrant when the Molotov-Ribbentrop Pact was initialed in August 1939. A few days later the Wehrmacht plunged into Poland from four directions while the Red Army remained poised on Poland's eastern frontier to make their move at the appropriate time. Hitler gambled that Britain and France would do nothing and that neither would get much encouragement from the United States.

Hitler's judgment was correct. Britain and France declared war but refused to fight it. The RAF dropped propaganda leaflets instead of bombs on Germany, and Hitler's first war directive enjoined the German troops on the western frontier to treat any action on France's part as a purely local matter. After Poland fell four weeks later, Hitler appealed to the Western Allies to make peace. Due to public indignation at Hitler's continuing audacity and not wishing to appear even more foolish by declaring war and then making peace without hardly firing a shot in anger against the enemy, the British and

French hoped to avoid conflict in their own sphere of influence while at the same time they hastily and belatedly prepared for such an eventuality. Meanwhile, the United States passed another Neutrality Act into law as public figures like Senators Borah, Taft and Wheeler toured the country like the famous aviator, Charles A Lindbergh, urging the country to put 'America First' and avoid the conflict at all costs. World War II was depicted as another 'of those age-old European struggles' which ought not to concern Americans. Although the America Firsters were branded as being Nazi sympathizers (which to a limited degree a man like Lindbergh, who had accepted the Order of the German Eagle from Goering only a couple of years before, was), almost all of them echoed a sincerely patriotic belief that was shared by most of their countrymen. They believed that it did not really matter who dominated Europe, Britain, France or Germany. Although radio agitator, Father Coughlin, actually preached anti-Semitism on a nation-wide hookup every week, he represented the view of a tiny minority of Americans. The majority, in both political parties, did not want to go to war. Their view was only slightly shaken when Britain and France were given little choice in the spring of 1940.

It may seem strange to Europeans today that in an election year, 1940, both major candidates, President Roosevelt and Wendell Willkie, both of whom privately sympathized with the Allied cause, should conduct a presidential election campaign trying to outdo the other in pandering to the isolationist vote. But that is precisely what happened throughout the year in which Denmark, Norway, Holland, Luxemburg, Belgium and France were overrun and in which Greece was invaded by the Italians. Although Britain's fighting spirit was finally aroused when Churchill became Prime Minister on the day that the Low Countries and France were invaded, it was sufficient only to 'win' the Battle of Britain. This time Hitler had misjudged one of his enemies. To the last he believed that Britain would make peace with Germany once France had fallen. When it became clear that Britain's pride, once challenged, would not submit to his will, he belatedly and unsuccessfully planned Operation Sea Lion, the scheme to invade Britain, which was ill-prepared and unrealistic; Germany simply lacked the naval strength to carry an invasion force across the English Channel even if the RAF had not stood up to the challenge of the Luft-waffe so heroically. Winning the Battle of Britain simply meant that Britain did not lose the war there and then. But as Churchill admitted to Roosevelt, Britain had no hope of reversing the series of Nazi victories without massive aid from the United States. Churchill did not openly admit that without massive *Soviet* aid Germany could not be defeated either.

So a holding operation began in the Atlantic, in North Africa and, to a lesser extent, in the Far East, until a change in the seemingly hopeless situation would take place. The destroyer-base deal between the United States and Great Britain in September 1940 made little difference and was useful largely for propaganda purposes rather than for maritime reasons. The Lend-Lease Act, passed by Congress with a majority of one vote, helped Britain rather more substantially. But direct American involvement in the war was not to be allowed by US public opinion even after ships of the US Navy were sunk in Atlantic waters and an undeclared naval war ensued between the US Navy and the Kriegsmarine. Respite only came when Hitler, overconfident from his victories of 1939 and 1940 as well as his more recent conquest of Greece in the spring of 1941, decided that a quick conquest of the Soviet Union would bring an end to the war he had already thought was won. The invasion of Russia as well as the unnecessary step of declaring war against the United States after Pearl Harbor when it was still possible that the Americans would have concentrated their efforts on defeating Japan to the exclusion of a European involvement were Hitler's undoing. He had attained power through bluff and intimidation. He conquered Europe, first by words and then with arms, with a force which was at all times demonstrably weaker than the combined forces of his enemies. Perhaps he was like a lucky gambler, who, having won with a small stake time and time again, decides to risk all on one final throw of the dice and loses. Perhaps he felt that the legacy of World War I, disillusionment, which brought him to power in Germany in the first place, and underlying racism and anti-Semitism, which he openly espoused and which all his enemies, including the Soviet Union, covertly shared, would make it possible for him to sweep all before him. His assumptions, which proved right so many times in the past, were finally proven wrong by that which had been the principal reason for his attaining power in Germany: national pride. Britain, Soviet Russia and the United States, like every country in the world, worshipped the arcane, pagan religion of the 20th century, nationalism, of which the swastika was the apotheosis. But it was meaningful only to the Germans and Austrians. His attempt to make it into an international banner through the Waffen SS, fell on stony soil throughout Europe, despite the thousands who rushed to join in the fight against Bolshevism and despite the efforts of the Norwegian Quisling, the Dutch Mussert and the French Laval and Pétain to reconcile their people to German hegemony in Europe. Once aroused, British, Russian and American national pride was as deep-seated as German nationalism. National feeling outweighed any other consideration which might have worked to Hitler's advantage. Hitler's chief error was in goading his potential enemies into arousing the spirit of nationalism among their peoples. And in this way Adolf Hitler, who took up the sword of nationalism to attain power in Germany and to expand German power throughout Europe, died by it. It is a tragedy that his philosophy of race hatred and anti-Semitism did not die with him.

Below: Hitler opens the autobahn in Silesia near the Czech border in 1936.

Hitler's Headquarters

Hitler's last years were spent in essentially three places: the Wolf's Lair, the Berghof at Berchtesgaden, and the Bunker under the Reichschancellery where Hitler finally met his death. His contacts were necessarily limited, and Martin Bormann made sure that they were.

Left: Goebbels (saluting), Robert Ley and Dr Frick meet Hitler in the summer of 1944 after the bomb plot.
Below left: The Shadow Krause and von Puttkammer after a meeting with the Führer in September 1944.
Below: Sepp Dietrich, Hitler's Waffen-SS commander, commiserates with the Führer in August 1944.
Right: Gauleiters meet with Hitler in the Wolf's Lair in August 1944.

Below: Hitler dines with his mistress Eva Braun. The picture on the right is captioned as the last one ever taken of him. This picture actually dates from late 1944/early 1945. It is also evident that the pictures are faked as the left one clearly shows a join.

DAS LETZTE BILD

Einen sensationellen Fund machten Angestellte des CIC (Counter Intelligence Corps) bei Zell am See bei der Mutter eines ehemaligen SS-Führers. Sie fanden dort ehemaliges Eigentum von Frau Eva Hitler geb. Braun, darunter ein Photoalbum mit Bildern von ihr. (Unsere Aufnahme zeigt sie beim Frühstück an der Seite Hitlers.)

Photo: AP

The Bomb Plot

On 20 July 1944 an attempt was made on Hitler's life in the Wolf's Lair in East Prussia. Planned for years and engendered largely by German officers who realized that unless Hitler was deposed Germany would be utterly destroyed, it almost worked. The bomb was placed under a heavy wooden table where Hitler was speaking, but seconds before it exploded, Hitler moved a few feet down the table. Hitler was wounded in the hand and badly shaken. Otherwise he was all right and was able to greet Mussolini who happened to be arriving later that day. Those who conspired to kill him were ruthlessly executed, and others who were not directly involved, like Rommel, who was aware that the plot was on, were forced to commit suicide.

Above: Hitler and Mussolini examine the damage done to the barracks by the bomb.
Below: Bormann and Goering examine the table where Hitler stood.

Above: Hitler greets Mussolini on his arrival in Rastenburg soon after the attempt on Hitler's life. Il Duce's visit was planned weeks before, but Hitler was able to greet him despite the attempt on his life.

Above: The two dictators have a chance to laugh at Hitler's luck at escaping death. Hitler believed that fate had preserved his life so that he could lead Germany to victory.

Above: Hitler covers his injured arm by a cloak as Himmler escorts him back to the Wolf's Lair, followed by Mussolini and Goering. His injuries were more severe than he and his advisors acknowledged

Above: Mussolini, Doenitz, Hitler, Goering and Fegelein watch Hitler's dog Blondie outside the Wolf's Lair on 20 July. Hitler holds his injured hand showing some pain.

The Final Days

As the ring around Berlin closed inexorably, Hitler chose to remain in the capital and meet his death there. Children were recruited to defend the capital, and with the Waffen-SS and Wehrmacht they held on with indefatigable fanaticism for many weeks before Russian troops stood in the garden of the Reichschancellery at the grave of Hitler and Eva Braun, whom he married just before they committed suicide on 30 April 1945.

Bottom right: Hitler discusses the defense of Berlin with his staff in the Bunker under the Reichschancellery.
Extreme left: Hitler shakes hands with young defenders of Berlin.
Left: Members of the Hitler Youth who won the Iron Cross in March 1945.
Right: Hitler awards the Iron Cross to a young recruit.
Below: Russian tanks pour into Berlin as the street-by-street battle continues.

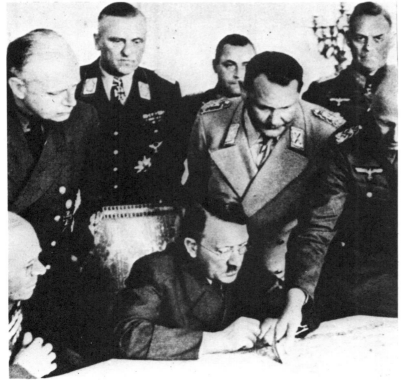

Above: The remains of part of Hitler's Bunker.
Left: Hitler, in a rare photograph showing him wearing glasses, in the Bunker with von Ribbentrop, Goering, Jodl and Keitel.
Right: German civilians view the Hitlerbunker after the city was overrun.
Extreme right: Part of the remains of the Bunker under the Reichs-chancellery.

HITLER'S
HOME

The remains of the Berghof in Berchtesgaden in Bavaria which was captured by the Americans. The Adolf-Hitlerstrasse leading to it was renamed the USA-Strasse. Some Germans in the neighborhood call it the 'Unser-Seelige-Adolfstrasse' ('our beloved Adolf Street').

Bundesarchiv provided all of the photographs in this book except for the following:

Bison Books: 1, 2/3, 4/5, 6/7 (all 3), 8 (all 3), 12, 14 (bottom right), 20/21 (top), 22 (bottom), 23 (both), 32 (top right), 34/35 (all 6), 36/37 (all 6), 38 (top right), 59 (bottom 3), 64 (bottom left), 65, 66/67 (all 6), 68/69, 70/71, 72 (both), 78 (bottom right), 79 (bottom 2), 80 (all 4), 89 (right 3), 90, 92,95 (right), 97, 116, 122/123 (top 3), 124 (top and bottom left), 125 (all 3), 126 (left 3 and bottom right), 139 (all 3), 140/141 (top 3), 142 (top), 143 (all 3), 145 (bottom right), 146 (both), 147 (top 3 and bottom left), 148/149, 149 (bottom), 153 (bottom left and right), 158 (top), 159 (both), 162 (top left), 170/171 (top 4), 172 (left 3), 177 (center right), 186, 188/189 (all 4), 192, 224 (top right), 228 (top 2 and bottom left), 229, 233 (both), 234/235 (all 4), 236/237, 238/239 (all 7), 245,

K W Krause: 32 (top left), 64 (top 2), 73 (top), 77 (top), 78 (bottom left and center left), 79 (top), 83 (center right), 117, 126 (top right), 130 (bottom), 134 (top left), 135, 136 (top left), 144 (top left and bottom), 147 (bottom right), 149 (top right, center right and inset bottom), 162/163 (bottom), 163 (top left), 194 (all 3), 195 (top 3), 204 (top right, center right and bottom), 222/223 (bottom), 223 (top right), 228 (bottom right), 246 (center left and bottom), 247 (bottom), 248 (center left).

H Walter: 124 (bottom right), 127.
Novosti Press Agency: 250/251 (bottom).
Robert Hunt Library: 196 (bottom right), 226 (top).
United States Air Force: 240 (top).
Presse-Illustrationen Heinrich Hoffman: 225 (top).
Herbert Hoffman: 133 (bottom left).
Paul Popper: 121